بِسۡمِ ٱللَّهِ ٱلرَّحۡمَٰنِ ٱلرَّحِيمِ

First published 2021

www.qiraatsimplified.com

Author Mohamed-Umer Esmail
Content Editor Saaima Yacoob
General Editor Syed Junaid Tayyab

Cover Design Huzaifa Saleh

تَسْهِيلُ الرُّسُوم

The Writing of the Qurʾān Simplified: *A Reader on the Collection and Orthography of the Qurʾān*

by Mufti Mohamed-Umer Esmail (d. 1441 AH)

Edited and Published Posthumously

Table of Contents

Editors' Foreword...5
Introduction...7
Development of Arabic Writing...10
The Sequence of the Arabic Alphabet...22
The Collection of the Qur'ān...25
Various Divisions of the Qur'ān...33
The Importance of Rasm al-Khaṭṭ...39
Arabic Khaṭṭ Throughout History...44
Books on Rasm al-Khaṭṭ...46
Principles of Rasm al-Khaṭṭ...49
Ḥadhf حذف...51
Ziyādah الزيادة...69
Ibdāl الإبدال...75
Waṣl and Faṣl وصل و فصل...78
Rules for Writing Hamza According to Rasm ʿUthmāni...95
Bibliography...98

Editors' Foreword

Over the last decade, the author of this text, Qārī Mufti Mohamed-Umer Esmail ﵀, taught the sciences of *tajwīd* and *qirā'āt* to students all over the world. While teaching his students, Mufti Mohamed-Umer Esmail ﵀ compiled both written and audio commentary in English on the texts and subjects he taught. His work benefited students by providing them access to this branch of sacred knowledge. Spanning over 700 pages, his commentaries are line-by-line translations and explanations of hundreds of lines of poetry and utilize dozens of sources and techniques to elucidate the vast and complex sciences of *tajwīd* and *qirā'āt*. For the non-scholar and non-Arabic speaker, this work is a blessing.

While he had the intention of publishing his works, his humility always led him to question whether his works were ready. We are honored to have the privilege of publishing his works which we have named:

Tashīl al-Jazariyyah

Tashīl al-Shāṭibiyyah

Tashīl al-Durrah

Tashīl al-Rusūm

We pray that these texts benefit both teachers and students of the Qur'ān around the world and serve as a continued source of *ṣadaqah jāriyah* for our beloved teacher ﵀. *Āmīn.*

As Imām al-Shāṭibī ﵀ states in his seminal text, *Ḥirz al-Amānī wa Wajh al-Tahānī* (commonly known as *al-Shāṭibiyah),*

جَزَى اللهُ بِالْخَيْرَاتِ عَنَّا أئمة لَنَا نَقَلُو الْقُرْآنَ عَذْبًا وَسَلْسَلَا

"May Allah grant abundant rewards on our behalf to the Imams who relayed to us the Qurʾān authenticated and precise."

Lastly, we request the generous reader to assign all errors to the editors as it was our responsibility to edit the works left to us by our teacher for any typing errors or unfinished content. The author did not consider these works ready for publishing during his lifetime. If you find any errors, please email them to us at info@qiraatsimplified.com.

With a request for *duʿās*,
Students of the late Mufti Mohamed-Umer Esmail ﷺ,

Junaid Tayyab
Sulma Badrudduja
Saaima Yacoob

Introduction

All praise is due to Allah, Most High who has preserved every aspect of His book, even its manner of writing, and may the peace and blessings of Allah be upon His beloved Prophet ﷺ, his family and his companions ﷦.

The work before you is a compilation of Mufti Mohamed-Umer Esmail's ﷦ teaching notes on the science of *Rasm* or Qur'ānic Orthography. Our respected teacher used to dedicate a few weeks to teach us various aspects of *Rasm* before he would teach us *al-Muqaddimah al-Jazariyyah*. This short work exposes a student to important topics related to the writing of the Qur'ān such as the development of the Arabic script, the compilation of the Qur'ān, early books written in the science of *Rasm*, as well as discussions around the principles of *Rasm* in a simple and accessible way. Like all books of this nature, this work should be studied with a teacher.

While this book is not a comprehensive text on the science of *Rasm*, it is an excellent introduction to it. It helps a student to place discussions about *Rasm* in their broader context and understand why certain words in the Qur'ān may be written the way they are. After going through this work, a student would better understand the two chapters related to *Rasm* in *al-Muqaddimah al-Jazariyyah*. For students of *qirā'āt*, this work serves as an important resource to understand the connection between the science of *Rasm* and the science of *Qirā'āt*.

In addition to the above, this work prepares students to begin their study of a text that goes through both the *uṣūl* and the *furūsh* of this science as well as the *ikhtilāfāt* between the ʿUthmānī codices. This work does not differentiate between the *uṣūl* and *furūsh* of the science of *Rasm*. Rather, it presents the reader with various examples, some that are covered under the *uṣūl* and others under the *furūsh*. The aim is always to show the reader a variety of words that are written uniquely in the orthography of the

Qur'ān, so that when he/she comes across them, he/she is better able to understand why they may have been written in this way.

As this work is a compilation of various chapters, understanding their placement is beneficial. As the Qur'ān was revealed in Arabic, the first two chapters explore the development of the Arabic script and the conventions added to it to facilitate the correct reading of the Qur'ān. The chapter that follows moves into the collection of the Qur'ān as the science of *Rasm* and its development is directly connected to this process. After the compilation of the whole Qur'ān, the *ummah*, at various intervals, added divisions in the Qur'ān to facilitate its recitation, such as *ajzā'*, *aḥzāb*, etc. These are explained in the chapter on "Various Divisions of the Qur'ān." The work then begins to discuss the science of *Rasm* and its significance. This is followed by a chapter on Arabic calligraphic scripts to remove any confusion between *Rasm al-khaṭṭ* and Arabic calligraphy. The next chapter lists the early books written in the science of *Rasm* as the reader would encounter some of the names of these scholars in the books and texts of *Rasm*. Next, the sources of the science of *Rasm* are listed, and then the work includes a chapter for each of the principles of *Rasm*.

While compiling our teacher's notes, I have corrected typing errors, as well as added references and explanatory footnotes where needed. Where I have added words directly into the text, I have placed them within square brackets. In the second half of the book, the reader will notice that not every example or explanation has been referenced. However, I have checked the examples as well as the various explanations that the esteemed author has given against books on the *rasm* of the Qur'ān. I mainly relied on the following five books when editing the second half of the book: *Sharḥ Matn ʿAqīlah Atrāb al-Qaṣā'id fī al-Rasm al-Qur'ānī* by Shaykh ʿAbd al-Fattāḥ al-Qāḍī, *Ashal al-Mawārid fī Sharḥ ʿAqīlah Atrāb al-Qaṣā'id* by Hazrat Qārī Fatḥ Muḥammad Pānīpatī, *Tashīl al-Bayān fī Rasm Khaṭṭ al-Qur'ān* by Qārī Nadhr Muḥammad, *Samīr al-Ṭālibīn* by Shaykh ʿAlī al-Ḍabbāʿ

and *Maʿrifah al-Rusūm* by Qārī Ibn Ḍiyāʾ Aḥmad. This last book also served as the inspiration for the title of this work.

I would like to thank my student, Basil Farooq, for his help in looking for references and his valuable feedback on the completed draft, and my student, Humayra Khan, for helping to proofread the electronic copy for any typesetting errors. May Allah reward them both and every person who advised us and made *duʿāʾ* for this work. *Āmīn.*

I ask Allah ﷻ to forgive us for our shortcomings, and to overlook our mistakes, and to accept this work from us and from our dear teacher, Mufti Mohamed-Umer Esmail ﷺ. *Āmīn.*

اللّٰهم هذا الدعاء وعليك الإجابة، وهذا الجهد وعليك التكلان

Saaima Yacoob
November 2021/Rabīʿ al-Thānī 1443

The Science of Rasm al-Khaṭṭ

Before studying the science of *rasm al-khaṭṭ*, it is imperative to know a brief history of the Arabic language.

Development of Arabic Writing

The Qurʾān consists of 114 chapters. The word used for each chapter of the Qurʾān is سُورَة written in English as *sūrah/sūra*. Its plural is سُوَر *suwar*. These *suwar* consist of verses/passages. The word used for verse is آيَة *āyah/āyat*. The plurals for *āyah* are آيات *āyāt* or آيٌ *āy*. A verse can be a full sentence, a part of a sentence, or it could consist of multiple sentences. Though the word "verse" is prevalently used for *āyah*, it is not the correct representation because a verse is a line of poetry and the Qurʾān is not poetry.

The word for sentence in Arabic is جُمْلَة *jumlah/jumla*. Its plural is *jumal* جُمَل. A *jumla* consists of words. The word used for words in Arabic is *kalimah* كَلِمَة. Its plural is *kalimāt*. A word consists of letters. The Arabic for letters is حَرْف *ḥarf*. Its plural is حُروف *ḥurūf*. The *ḥarf* or letter is the smallest component of what composes the Qurʾān.

The word *ḥarf* literally means a corner, side, or border. It is also used to mean a method or mode. Since letters in Arabic fall on the side of their names, they are named *ḥarf / ḥurūf*. For example the letter ص when spelled out is صاد. The actual letter falls at the beginning of its name which is also the side of its name, thus getting the name *ḥarf*. The same is the case with the rest of the letters except *alif* and *hamza*. *Alif* is an exception because *alif* being a letter of *madd* (long vowel) cannot possibly be at the beginning of a word, thus *alif* was named with *hamza* at the beginning due to the similarity of both their shape and *makhraj*. Mubarrad the famous grammarian considered *hamza* and *alif* both as one letter.[1] As for *hamzah*, in reality it was *amzah*.[2] It is common in Arabic to change the *hā*ʾ to *hamza* and vice versa. For example, ماء originally was ماه.[3]

Technically, the word *ḥarf* is used for different meanings in different sciences. In the science of Arabic grammar, *ḥarf* can refer to a letter and also to a particle or preposition i.e., a word that is neither a noun nor a verb and cannot convey its full meaning on its own. In the science of *qirāʾāt*, it refers to a word of the Qurʾān that can be recited in different ways as long as it is in accordance with the rules of Arabic grammar and *ʿUthmānī rasm al-khaṭṭ* and its transmission is *mutawātir*. The word *ḥarf* is also used for a particular dialect or accent of a people.

When the Qurʾān was being revealed, it would immediately be written. The letters were empty of dots. The Arabs were sufficiently skilled in their language to be able to discern the letters without dots, also using the context of the writing. Some have written that the use of dots was considered a sign of weakness and ignorance of the language. It was considered an insult if someone received a letter with dots.[4] There were a total of 18 letters that were used to pronounce the 29 letters of the Arabic alphabet as we know it today. The 18 letters were:

ا ٮ ح د ر س ص ط ع ڡ ٯ ک ل م ں ه و ى

[1] Iẓhār Thānwī, *al-Jawāhir al-Naqiyyah*, 24.

[2] Mullā ʿAlī al-Qārī, *al-Minaḥ al-Fikriyyah*, 72.

[3] Iẓhār Thanwī, *al-Jawāhir al-Naqiyyah*, 24.

[4] Usmani, *An Approach to the Qurʾānic Sciences*, 206; Qalqashandī, *Ṣubḥ al-Aʿshā fī Ṣanāʿah al-Inshā*ʾ, 3:149.

The Introduction of Dots

The word *naqṭ* نَقْط in Arabic means to draw dots and technically it means to write diacritical points or marks. *Nuqṭah* نُقْطَة means one dot and its plural is نُقَط *nuqaṭ*. There are two types of *naqṭ*; *Naqṭ al-iʿjām* نَقْط الإعْجام and *naqṭ al-iʿrāb* نَقْط الإعراب.

Naqṭ al-iʿrāb was used for the short vowels i.e., *ḍammah*, *fatḥah*, *kasrah*, and for the absence of a vowel i.e., *sukūn* and for nunation i.e., *tanwīn*. In the beginning dots were marked on the top, bottom, behind or in front of words to denote the short vowels on words.[5]

Naqṭ al-iʿjām refers to the dots used on letters to distinguish between those letters that have identical shapes.

The History of *Naqṭ al-Iʿrāb* نَقْط الإعراب

During the *khilāfah* of Muʿāwiyah ibn Abī Sufyān ﵁, he wrote to Ziyād—who was the governor of Baṣrah—summoning his son ʿUbaid Allah ibn Ziyād. When he entered upon Muʿāwiyah ﵁, Muʿāwiyah ﵁ noticed that he was erring in his speech. On this Muʿāwiyah ﵁ wrote to Ziyād reprimanding him on his son's erring in speech. Ziyād sent for the well-known scholar of the time Abū al-Aswad al-Duʾalī and said to him, "These non-Arabs have distorted the Arabic language. Why don't you create something through which people can correct their speech and accurately recite the Word of Allah?" Abū al-Aswad declined and went away.

Ziyād was not one to give up. He asked a person to sit in the path of Abū al-Aswad and deliberately recite the Qurʾān incorrectly. When Abū al-Aswad passed by this person, he heard him recite the first verse of *Sūrah*

---

[5] Shafi Usmani, *Maʿārif al-Qurʾān*, 1:32.

al-Barāʾah incorrectly, in a manner that would mean that Allah has nothing to do with the polytheists and His Prophet, when it should be Allah and His Prophet have nothing to do with the polytheists. Abū al-Aswad found that repugnant and said, "Allah is above having nothing to do with His Prophet," and right away returned to Ziyād and accepted his request and said that he will begin with the *iʿrāb* (*ḍammah*, *fatḥah*, *kasrah* etc.) of the Qurʾān. He asked Ziyād to send him thirty scholars so that he can choose one of them to help him in his cause. Ziyād sent thirty scholars to him and Abū al-Aswad continued to test them until he chose one scholar who was from the tribe of Banū ʿAbd al-Qais.

Abū al-Aswad said to him: Grab the *muṣḥaf* and some ink of a color different from the color of the *muṣḥaf* and listen carefully to me. Whenever you find me opening my mouth while reciting a letter, place a dot on top of that letter, and when you see me rounding my lips, place a dot in front of the letter, and when you see me lowering them, write a dot underneath the letter. As for when you see me following up with a *ghunnah* sound (*nūn* sound as in *tanwīn*), write two dots (instead of one) appropriately. As for the letter without a vowel (*sākin*) leave it without dots.[6]

Every time a page was completed, Abū al-Aswad would double check it with him until they completed the whole *muṣḥaf* likewise.

Scribes during the time of Abū al-Aswad and thereafter continued to follow suit and some made slight changes to the dots. Some adopted a small square in place of a dot, some adopted a small filled in circle and some adopted a small unfilled circle. The people of Madinah introduced the breve (˘) for *mushaddad* letters and the macron (‾) for *sukūn*. This is how it was until the end of the Umayyad (Banū Umayyah) leadership.

---

[6] Al-Qāḍī, *Tārīkh al-Muṣḥaf al-Sharīf*, 44.

Later dots were introduced to distinguish letters from their look-alikes. Naturally this caused confusion between the two sets of dots, dots for the *ḥarakāt* and dots for the letters. Also, it was becoming tedious for many to write the Qurʾān with one color ink and the dots with another color. Hence, during the Abbasid period, a scholar by the name of Khalīl ibn Aḥmad al-Farāhīdī introduced a diacritical system quite different and more elaborate than the one introduced by Abū al-Aswad. Instead of dots, he used the letter from which each of the short vowels is created, but in a much more diminutive shape. [7] He also introduced the shape ء for the letter *hamza.*[8] The diacritical marks he introduced were eight:[9]

1. *Fatḥah*: A mini *alif* horizontally placed over the letter. If a *nūn* is to be added as in *tanwīn* then two horizontal *alifs*. Later on, the *alif/s* were written diagonally.
2. *Kasrah*: A mini *yāʾ* in the shape (ـے) which later lost its arch and became like a horizontal *alif* under the letter. This would be doubled if the letter was nunated (*tanwīn*). This later was written diagonally as well.
3. *Ḍammah*: A mini *wāw* placed on top of the letter. This would be doubled in the case of *tanwīn*. This was written diagonally later on. The scholars of *al-maghrib* (the West) removed the circle part of the *wāw* for the *ḍammah*. Thus, making it look like a slanted د.
4. *Sukūn/Jazm*: A small *mīm* without the tail (ْ) on top of the letter alluding to the *mīm* in the word *jazm*. In some cases the head of the letter *jīm* (جـ) would be placed on top of the letter to allude to the *jīm* in *jazm*. The dot of the *jīm* was later dropped.
5. *Tashdīd/Shaddah*: A small letter *shīn* would be placed on top of the letter. The semi-circle part and the dots were later dropped.

[7] Shaʿbān Muḥammad Ismāʿīl, *Rasm al-Muṣḥaf wa Ḍabṭuhu*, 89.

[8] Al-Suyūṭī, *al-Itqān fī ʿUlūm al-Qurʾān*, 4:184; Shafī Usmānī, *Maʿārif al-Qurʾān*, 1:32.

[9] Al-Suyūṭī, *al-Itqān fī ʿUlūm al-Qurʾān*, 4:186. The first six diacritical marks are mentioned here.

6. *Hamza al-Qaṭʿ*: The head of the letter *ʿain* reduced in size (ء) was used to represent *hamza al-qaṭʿ*. Sometimes it would be on its own, sometimes on top of *alif*, sometimes underneath it, sometimes on *wāw* and sometimes on *yāʾ* depending on the circumstances.
7. *Hamza al-Waṣl*: The head of the letter *ṣād* (صـ) was placed on top of *alif* to allude that it is connected with the word before it. This sign is not used in the South Asian prints of the Qurʾān prevalent today.
8. *Madd*: The word *madd* (مد) was written on top of the letter to be stretched. Later, the circle part of the *mīm* and top part of the *dāl* was removed to form ~.

Naqṭ al-Iʿjām نَقْط الإعجام

Although diacritical points for letters existed during pre-Islamic times, they were rarely used.[10] They were not incorporated in the earliest manuscripts of the Holy Qurʾān. During the reign of Banu Umayyah, under the leadership of ʿAbd al-Malik ibn Marwān, the fifth Umayyad *khalīfah*, it was feared that due to non-Arab integration, the Arabic language would lose its original essence and beauty, and hence lead to distortion in the recitation of the Qurʾān.

ʿAbd al-Malik ibn Marwān ordered Ḥajjāj ibn Yūsuf—the governor of ʿIrāq—to rectify the situation. Ḥajjāj ibn Yūsuf asked Naṣr ibn ʿĀṣim al-Laithī—the student of Abū al-Aswad al-Duʾalī—and Yaḥyā ibn Yaʿmur al-ʿAdwānī—both from the *tābiʿīn*—to take care of this.[11]

So, both of them devised a convention that distinguished the letters with the same shape from one another. The first thing they introduced was the dots for *bāʾ*, *tāʾ* and *thāʾ*. They placed one dot under *bāʾ* as it was the first letter, two dots on *tāʾ* as it was the second letter and three dots on top of

---

[10] Al-Azami, *The History of the Qurʾānic Text*, 151-156.

[11] Ṭāsh Kubrā Zādā, *Miftāḥ al-Siyādah*, 2:21; al-Qāḍī, *Tārīkh al-Muṣḥaf al-Sharīf*, 45.

*thā*ʾ as it was the third letter. Then they placed the letters that resembled one another in pairs and left the first one without a dot and placed one dot on top of the second as in غ ع ط ظ س ش ص ض د ذ ر ز. Thus, the *Hijāʾī* or *Alif Bāʾī* order was created.[12]

As for the letter *shīn* it was feared that it may create confusion between its medial form and *nūn's* medial form, so they placed three dots horizontally on it; one on top of each tooth of the three teeth (upward facing small lines) of the letter *shīn*. In the *muṣḥafs* printed in the West (North Africa and Spain region), till today the letter *shīn* has three dots placed horizontally on the *shīn*, while the East later on changed this to three dots placed in a triangular form on top of *shīn*.

As for the letters ج ح خ they decided to place one dot in the middle of *jīm*, one dot on top of *khā*ʾ and nothing on *ḥā*ʾ.

As for ق and ف they decided to keep one dot for *qāf* on top and one dot for *fa*ʾ at the bottom. Keep in mind that the bottom part of both letters was the same. The *muṣḥafs* of Maghrib even today follow this convention for *fā*ʾ and *qāf*. The East later on adopted the convention of two dots on top for *qāf* and one dot on top for *fā*ʾ.

As for ص ض ط ظ in their medial forms, they decided to add an extra small tooth after ص and ض as in صـ and ضـ and a longer one on top of ط and ظ to alleviate confusion. To alleviate confusion between صـ and ط and between ضـ and ظ. The long tooth on top of ط and ظ was initially slightly closer to the middle. In some traditional books they will add the adjective المشالة after ط and ظ which means the one with an extra line on top.

---

[12] ʿUbaidāt, "*Aṣwāt al-ʿArabiyyah min al-Tartīb al-Abjadī ilā al-Tartīb al-Ṣawtī*," 175.

ك and ل in their initial and medial forms looked alike i.e. ـلـ and ـلـ. The sign ٕ that resembles ء was placed on top of *kāf* to distinguish it from *lām*. Later on, the line of the *kāf* was slanted and the sign became a slanted line as well e.g., ک ک. Some *muṣḥafs* today still have the antique method of writing *kāf*.

From the above we can conclude the following:

1. The first good innovation to take place in the *muṣḥaf ʿUthmānī* was the insertion of dots to denote the short vowels and its innovator was Abū al-Aswad al-Duʾalī. This was later replaced by the convention introduced by Khalīl ibn Aḥmad al-Farāhīdī.
2. Early manuscripts did not have dots for every single letter, rather only for those letters for which correct recitation was required.
3. The second good innovation was the introduction of dots to distinguish letters. Its innovators were Naṣr ibn ʿĀṣim and Yaḥyā ibn Yaʿmur.
4. The dots for the short vowels were innovated before the dots for the letters.
5. Initially the dots were written in a different color. This was gradually abandoned after the introduction of Khalīl's diacritical system.

The following diagram shows the evolution of the diacritical systems taken from Qurʾān manuscripts with Kūfī *khaṭṭ* from the 9th-11th centuries:[13]

[13] Yassine Mrabet, license CC BY-SA 4.0 Arabic diacritics - Wikipedia

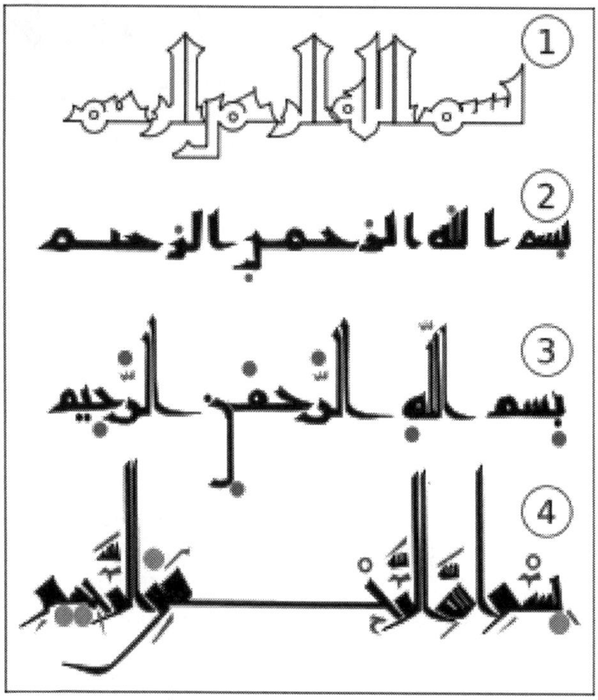

1. Early 9th century CE script with no dots or diacritic marks. Also see diagram number 1 for seventh century excerpt in Kufic script:
2. 9th - 10th century CE under the Abbasid dynasty, Abū al-Aswad's system established red dots with each arrangement or position indicating a different short vowel.
3. Later, a second system, using black dots, was used to differentiate between letters like *fāʾ* and *qāf*. Also see diagram number two below:
4. 11th century CE. In al-Farāhīdī's system (the system we know today), dots were changed into shapes resembling the letters to transcribe the corresponding long vowels. Also see diagram 3 below.

Diagram number 1

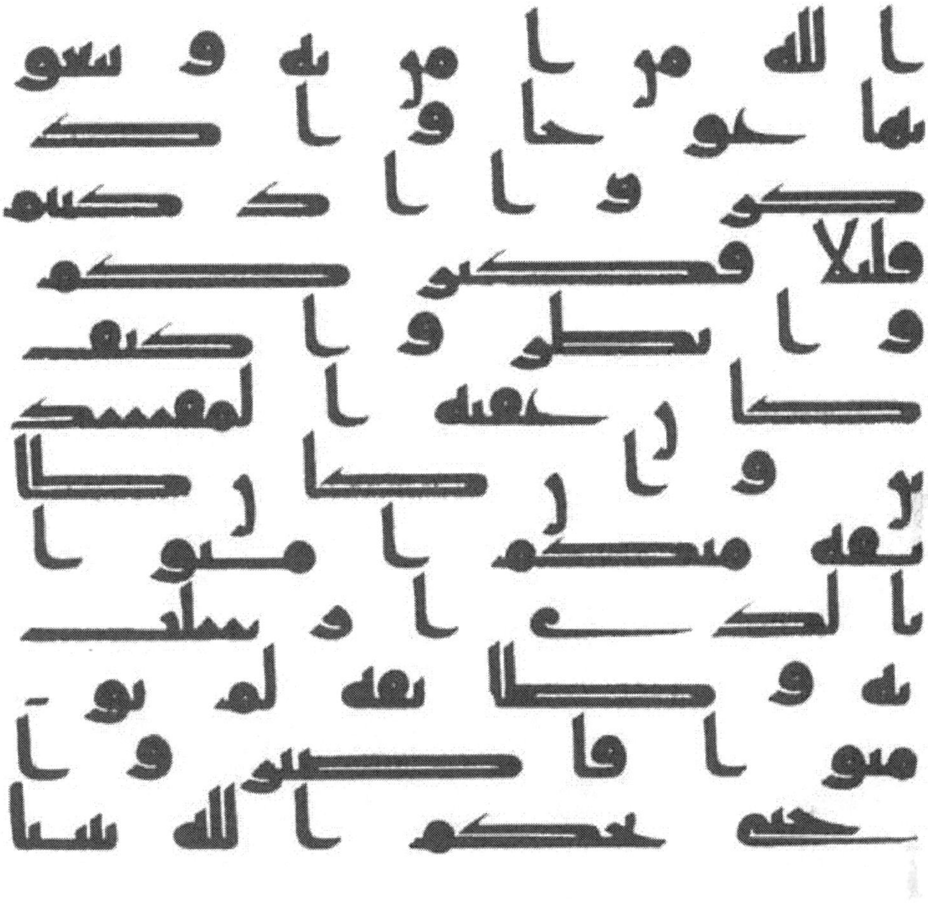

Kufic script, from an early Qurʾān manuscript showing Sūrah 7 (al-Aʿrāf) verses 86 & 87, 8th – 9th century. National Library, St. Petersburg, Russia.

Diagram number 2

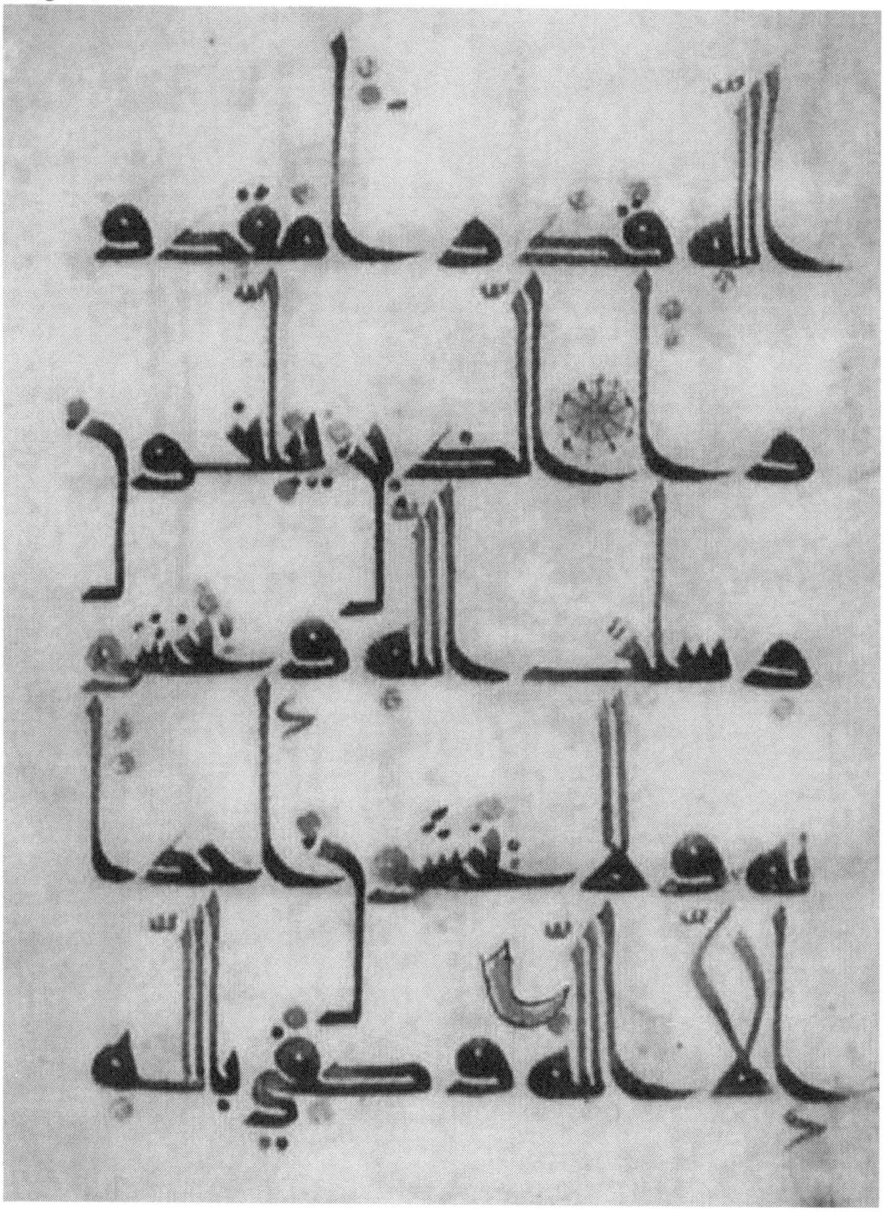

Diagram number 3

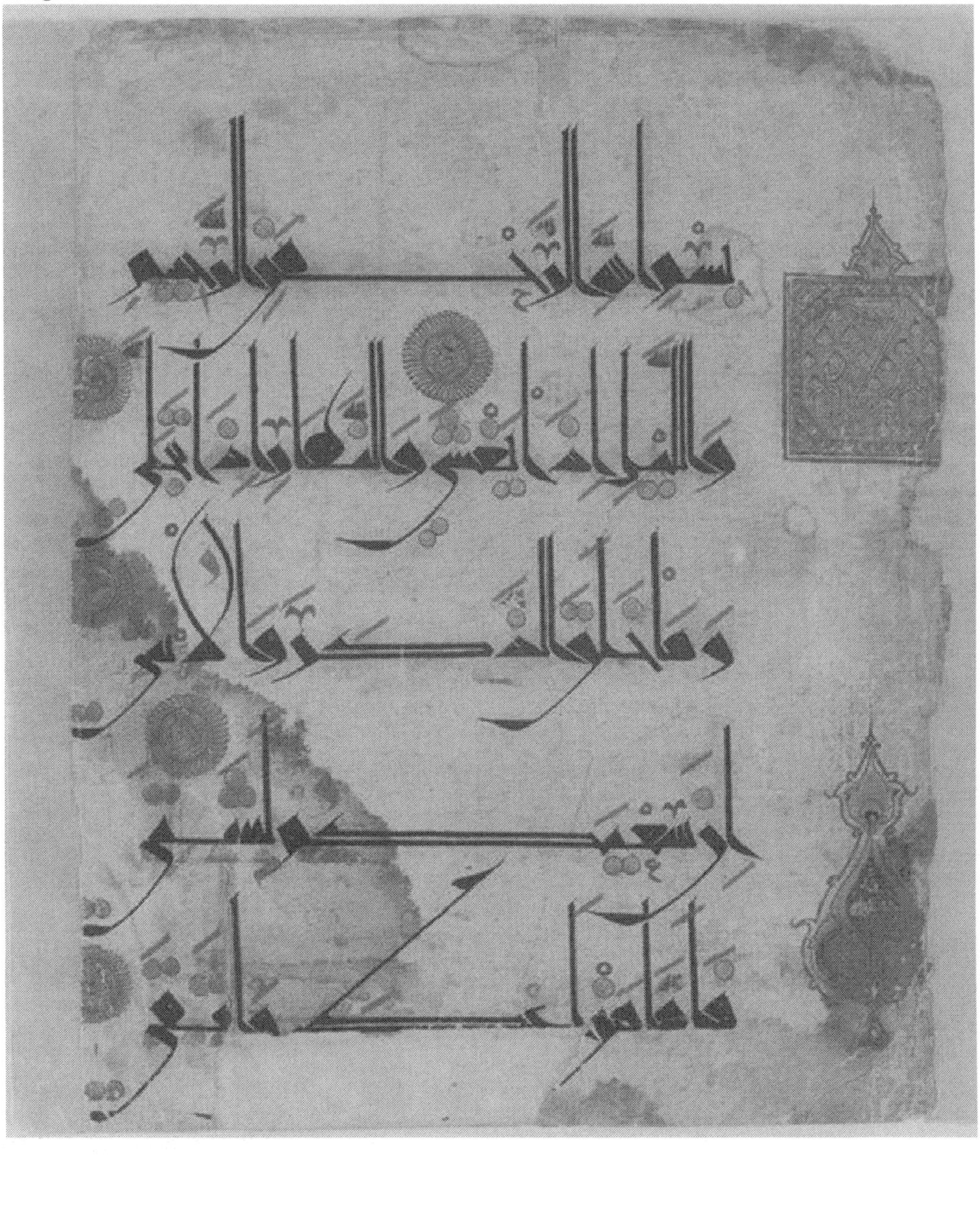

The Sequence of the Arabic Alphabet

The Arabs until the end of the first century *hijrī* used to pronounce the letter *hamza*, but they did not have a separate shape for it in writing.[14] When they would write a word with a *hamza* in it, depending on the spelling, they would sometimes borrow the letter *alif* e.g., when writing نَشَأَ they would write is as نشا and while reading they would read it with a *hamza* not an *alif*. They would sometimes use the letter *wāw* for *hamza*. For example, while writing يُؤْمِنُ, they would write it as يومن and read it with a *hamza* not a *wāw*. Sometimes they would borrow the letter *yā*ʾ for *hamza*, like in بِئْر. They would write it as بيبر, but pronounce it with a *hamza*.[15] Sometimes they would write a word with a *hamza* without using any letter for it. Examples are قُرْءان and سَماء. They would write them as قران and سما, but would pronounce the *hamza* anyways.

At the beginning of the second *hijrī* century, a scholar by the name of Khalīl ibn Aḥmad al-Farāhīdī borrowed the head of the *ʿain* and appointed it as the official shape for the letter *hamza*.[16] From then onwards, *hamza* became an official letter with a written form.

Therefore, the number of letters that are written will be one fewer than the number of letters that are pronounced due to *hamza* being the letter that is pronounced but not written. The Arabic letters that are written are known as *al-Ḥurūf al-Abjadiyyah* and they are 28, beginning with *alif* that is metaphorically called *hamza* because *alif* is borrowed to represent *hamza*.[17] The following are the *Abjad* letters:

---

[14] Ibn al-Jazarī, *al-Tamhīd*, 115.

[15] Ibn Ḍiyāʾ Muḥib al-Dīn Aḥmad, *Maʿrifah al-Rusūm*, 5-6.

[16] Shafī Usmānī, *Maʿārif al-Qurʾān*, 1:32.

[17] Al-Dānī, *al-Muḥkam*, 27.

ا ب ج د ه و ز ح ط ى ك ل م ن س ع ف ص ق ر ش ت ث خ ذ ض ظ غ

ابجد هوز حطى كلمن سعفص قرشت ثخذ ضظغ

The scholars of the West[18] had a slightly different order of *Abjad* letters:

ابجد هوز حطى كلمن صعفض قرست ثخذ ظغش

The Arabic letters that are pronounced are called *al-ḥurūf al-hijāʾiyyah. Hijāʾ* means to spell or pronounce the letters separately. They are 29, beginning with *hamza*, which is called *alif* metaphorically because whenever *hamza* comes at the beginning of a word, it is written as an *alif* or on top of it or underneath it.

أ ب ت ث ج ح خ د ذ ر ز س ش ص ض ط ظ ع غ ف ق ك ل م ن ه و لا ى

The *alif* was placed between *wāw* and *yāʾ* adjoined with *lām maftūḥa*—which is pronounced *lām-alif* or just *lā*—due to the fact that *alif* cannot be pronounced on its own (due to being a long vowel).

Another sequence of the Arabic letters is grouping them in terms of their *makhraj* (place of articulation). Thus, there are 3 orders of the Arabic alphabet:

1. الترتيب الهجائى The *Hijāʾī* order is also known as الترتيب الألفبائى. The *Alif-Bāʾ* order is also known as حروف الإعجام or الحروف المُعْجَمَة. The dotted letters or the letters that are pronounced separately. Imam Khalīl and his student named them الحروف العربية.
2. الترتيب الأبجدى The *Abjadi* Order
3. الترتيب الصوتى The *Makhraj* Order

[18] Refers to the scholars of Spain and North Africa.

Sometimes the letters are divided into الحروف المعجمة والمهملة, letters with dots and the letters without dots.

The letters with dots are:

ب ت ث ج خ ذ ز ش ض ظ غ ف ق ن ى

According to *Rasm ʿUthmāni*[19], there are five instances where the ى does not have dots:

1. When it is final (at the end of a word) e.g. مَحْيَاىَ
2. When it is a seat for *hamza* e.g. لِئَلَّا
3. When it is a replacement for a letter, mostly *alif*, or the more familiar term is *alif maqṣūrah* whether medial or final, e.g. وَٱلضُّحَىٰ ﴿١﴾
4. When it is brought in to indicate an omitted *yāʾ* in the *rasm*, e.g. إِۦلَٰفِهِمۡ
5. When it is brought in to indicate a *ṣilah* (long vowel), e.g. فَأَثَرۡنَ بِهِۦ نَقۡعٗا ﴿٤﴾

The letters without dots are:

أ ح د ر س ص ط ع ك ل م ه و

---

[19] *Rasm ʿUthmānī* refers to the divinely inspired writing of the Qurʾān. Here though, the author is using the term *rasm ʿUthmānī* to refer to the writing of the Qurʾān (with dots and vowel markings) as it is written in the *muṣāḥif* printed today in the Arab world.

The Collection of the Qurʾān

The collection of the Qurʾān in classical [books] is referred to as جمع القرآن. جمع القرآن can mean the memorization of the Qurʾān, its preservation, writing, documentation, and compilation into book form.[20]

Jamʿ of the Qurʾān can be categorized into three stages:

1. The era of the Messenger of Allah ﷺ
2. The *Jamʿ* of Abū Bakr ﵁
3. The *Jamʿ* of ʿUthmān ﵁

1. The Era of the Messenger of Allah ﷺ

Whenever an *āyah* or *sūrah* would be revealed, the Messenger of Allah ﷺ would call Zaid ﵁ and dictate it to him and he would write it down. It is reported in *Ṣaḥīḥ Bukhārī* narrated by al-Barāʾ: There was revealed 'Not equal are those believers who sit (at home) and those who strive and fight in the cause of Allah' (4:95). The Prophet ﷺ said: 'Call Zaid to me and let him bring the board, the ink pot and the scapula bone (or the scapula bone and the ink pot).' Then he ﷺ said: 'Write: Not equal are those believers ...[21]

Al-Suyūṭī in *al-Itqān* also mentions that the material upon which the revelation had been written down was kept in the house of the Prophet ﷺ.[22]

---

[20] Al-Masʾūl, *Muʿjam al-Muṣṭalaḥāt*, 164.

[21] Bukhārī, 4990, 4594.

[22] Al-Suyūṭī, *al-Itqān fī ʿUlūm al-Qurʾān*, 1:207.

Al-Ḥārith al-Muḥāsibī in his book *Kitāb Fahm al-Sunan*, summarized the first phase of the written collection of the Qurʾānic material in the following words:

"Writing of the Qurʾān was no novelty, for the Prophet used to order that it be written down, but it was in separate pieces, on scraps of leather, shoulder blades and palm risp,[23] and when (Abū Bakr) al-Ṣiddīq ordered that it be copied from the (various) places to a common place, which was in the shape of sheets, these (materials) were found in the house of the Prophet in which the Qurʾān was spread out, and he gathered it all together and tied it with a string so that nothing of it was lost.[24]

There were many other scribes that would write the revelation for the Messenger of Allah ﷺ.[25] The written revelation would be referred to as *ṣuḥuf* صُحُف plural of صَحِيفَة i.e., separated pieces of loose parchments of skin, bone, papyrus, paper or scrolls.

The following are some important points about the collection of the Qurʾān during the era of the Messenger of Allah ﷺ.

- The revelation was written down by many of the *ṣaḥāba* ﷻ. The revelation would be written on scraps of leather, shoulder blades and palm risp.
- Many had copies of the revelation, partially or wholly.
- All the *ṣaḥāba* ﷻ had portions memorized.
- Many had the entire Qurʾān memorized.
- The Messenger of Allah ﷺ himself instructed his scribes as to where the different revealed verses should be placed, and thus, determined the order and arrangement.

---

[23] Stalks

[24] Al-Suyūṭī, *Al-Itqān fī ʿUlūm al-Qurʾān*, 1:206-207.

[25] Shafī Usmānī, *Maʿārif al-Qurʾān*, 1:22.

- This order and arrangement were well known to the Muslims and strictly observed by them.

- Jibrīl 🕊 went through all the revelation with Muḥammad ﷺ each year in Ramadan, and went through it twice in the year the Messenger of Allah ﷺ passed away.

- There are numerous reports about the existence of the written Qurʾān in the form of a book or piece of writing (*kitāb*) during the lifetime of the Prophet ﷺ.

2. The Jamʿ of Abū Bakr ؓ

After the demise of the Messenger of Allah ﷺ, during the Caliphate (*khilāfah*) of Abū Bakr ؓ, a battle by the name of Yamāmah took place wherein many *qurrāʾ* (scholars of the Qurʾān) were martyred, thus creating the need to bring the Qurʾān together in one place. *Ṣaḥīḥ Bukhārī* relates this incident as follows:

Zaid ibn Thābit al-Anṣārī, one of the scribes of the Revelation narrates, "Abū Bakr sent for me after the martyrdom of many *qurrāʾ* during the battle of Yamāmah. ʿUmar was also present. Abū Bakr said, ʿUmar has come to me and said, 'the people have suffered heavy casualties on the day of (the battle of) Yamāmah, and I am afraid that there will be some casualties among the *qurrāʾ* (those who know the Qurʾān by heart) at other places, whereby a large part of the Qurʾān may be lost, unless you collect it. And I am of the opinion that you should collect the Qurʾān.' Abū Bakr added, 'I said to ʿUmar, "How can I do something which Allah's Apostle has not done?" ʿUmar said (to me) "By Allah, it is (really) a good thing." ʿUmar kept on insisting to accept his proposal, till Allah opened my heart for it and I agreed with ʿUmar'. (Zaid ibn Thābit added), ʿUmar was sitting with him (Abū Bakr) and was not speaking. Abū Bakr said (to me), 'You are a wise young man and we do not suspect you (of telling lies or of forgetfulness); and you used to write the Divine Revelation for the

Messenger of Allah ﷺ. Therefore, look for the Qur'ān and collect it (in one manuscript)'. By Allah, if he (Abū Bakr) had ordered me to shift one of the mountains (from its place) it would not have been harder for me than what he had ordered me concerning the collection of the Qur'ān. I said to both of them, 'How dare you do a thing which the Prophet has not done?' Abū Bakr said, 'By Allah, it is (really) a good thing. So I kept on arguing with him about it till Allah opened my heart for that which He had opened the hearts of Abū Bakr and 'Umar. So I started locating the Qur'ānic material and collecting it from parchments, scapula, leafstalks of date palms and from the memories of men (who knew it by heart). I found with Khuzaima two verses of *sūrah* al-Tauba which I had not found with anybody else (and they were):

'Verily there has come to you an Apostle (Muhammad) from among yourselves. It grieves him that you should receive any injury or difficulty. He (Muhammad) is ardently anxious over you (to be rightly guided).' (9:128)

The manuscript of the Qur'ān that was collected remained with Abū Bakr till Allah took him unto Him, and then with 'Umar till Allah took him unto Him, and finally it remained with Ḥafṣa, 'Umar's daughter.[26]

Zaid ibn Thābit and 'Umar ؓ set out to fulfill this daunting task and though they were both *ḥāfiẓ* (they both had the Qur'ān memorized) they did not rely solely on their memory, nor did they solely rely on the memories of the hundreds of other *ṣaḥāba* ؓ who had committed the Qur'ān to memory, nor did he rely solely on the already available manuscripts of the Qur'ān. Rather, they announced to all far and wide that whoever has any part of the Qur'ān memorized or in writing, they should

---

[26] Bukhārī, 4986.

bring it. They took the following steps before including any *āyah* in their collection:[27]

1. They verified it with their memory.
2. Two witnesses had to testify that the *āyah* was written in the presence of the Messenger of Allah ﷺ.[28]
3. It was collated with the collections that numerous *ṣaḥāba* رضي الله عنهم had in their possession.

Some distinctive features of this copy were:

- The *āyāt* were arranged in the order prescribed by the Messenger of Allah ﷺ.
- Each *sūrah* was written and kept separately.
- It was written in the Ḥīrī script.[29]
- The *āyāt* whose recital was abrogated were not included.
- It was endorsed by the entire Ummah at the time (*ijmāʿ*).
- It was named *al-Umm* (The Basis) so that it can serve as a reference point for all Muslims and further generations.

3. The *Jamʿ* of ʿUthmān رضي الله عنه

Islam had spread to other regions of the Middle East and Muslims continued to learn, recite and teach the Qurʾān knowing that the Qurʾān may be recited according to the seven known dialects. Gradually with their integration into the dialects other than the seven agreed upon dialects and their integration into non-Arab cultures and dialects, people

---

[27] Shafī Usmānī, *Maʿārif al-Qurʾān*, 1:24-25.

[28] Al-Suyūṭī, *al-Itqān fī ʿUlūm al-Qurʾān*, 1:205.

[29] Abū al-Ḥasan Aʿẓamī, introduction to *Tashīl al-Bayān fī Rasm Khaṭṭ al-Qurʾān* by Nadhar Muḥammad, 8.

started coming up with their own dialects in terms of reciting the Qurʾān. This has been outlined in the following Hadith of *Saḥīḥ Bukhārī*:

Anas ibn Mālik narrates: Ḥudhaifa ibn al-Yamān came to ʿUthmān at the time when the people of Shām and the people of ʿIrāq were waging war against Armenia and Azerbaijan. Ḥudhaifa was afraid of their (the people of Shām and ʿIrāq) differences in the recitation of the Qurʾān, so he said to ʿUthmān, 'O chief of the Believers! Save this nation before they differ about the Book (Qurʾān), as the Jews and the Christians did before.' So ʿUthmān sent a message to Ḥafṣa saying, 'Send us the manuscripts of the Qurʾān so that we may compile the Qurʾānic materials in perfect copies and return the manuscripts to you'. Ḥafṣa sent it to ʿUthmān. ʿUthmān then ordered Zaid ibn Thābit, ʿAbd Allah ibn al-Zubair, Saʿīd ibn al-ʿĀṣ and ʿAbd al-Raḥmān ibn Ḥārith ibn Hishām to rewrite the manuscripts in perfect copies. ʿUthmān said to the three Quraishī men, 'In case you disagree with Zaid ibn Thābit on any point in the Qurʾān, then write it in the dialect of Quraish as the Qurʾān was revealed in their tongue.' They did so, and when they had written many copies, ʿUthmān returned the original manuscripts to Ḥafṣa. ʿUthmān sent to every Muslim province one copy of what they had copied and ordered that all the other Qurʾānic materials whether written in fragmentary manuscripts or whole copies, be burnt. Zaid ibn Thābit added, 'A verse from *sūrah* al-Aḥzāb was missed by me when we copied the Qurʾān and I used to hear Allah's Apostle reciting it. So we searched for it and found it with Khuzaima ibn Thābit al-Anṣārī'. (That verse was): 'Among the Believers are men who have been true in their covenant with Allah' (33: 23).[30]

According to the well-known report, five *muṣḥafs* were sent to the major cities of the time, Makkah al-Mukarramah, Kūfah, Baṣrah, Shām and Madinah al-Munawwarah. ʿUthmān ﷺ also sent teachers along with these *muṣḥafs*. With the *muṣḥaf* kept for Madinah was appointed Zaid ibn Thābit

[30] Bukhārī, 4987, 4988.

﷽. Abū ʿAbd al-Raḥmān al-Sulamī ⁎ was sent with the *muṣḥaf* sent to Kūfa. ʿĀmir ibn ʿAbd Qais ⁎ was sent with the *muṣḥaf* of Baṣrah. Mughirah ibn Abī Shihāb ⁎ for the *muṣḥaf* of Shām and ʿAbd Allah ibn al-Sāʾib was sent with the *muṣḥaf* of Makkah.[31] ʿUthmān ⁎ had one *muṣḥaf* prepared for himself as well and that *muṣḥaf* is known as al-Imam. This is why some reports mention six *muṣḥafs* were prepared. Some have mentioned that a *muṣḥaf* was sent to Baḥrain and one was sent to Yemen.[32] Some have also claimed that one *muṣḥaf* was sent to Egypt.[33]

Each teacher was ordered to teach the Qurʾān to the surrounding localities according to the *muṣḥaf* they were sent with. In order to accommodate the mass-communicated, uninterrupted and universally accepted *qirāʾāt*, the *Shāmi muṣḥaf* and *Madanī muṣḥaf* had slight variances in a couple of places, for example in the *Shāmi muṣḥaf*, the word وصى is written as أوصى[34]

Some of the features of this compilation were:

1. The main purpose was to have the entire Ummah adopt one script for the writing, learning, teaching and propagation of the Holy Qurʾān.
2. The *sūrahs* were arranged in their present order.
3. To accommodate the mass-communicated, uninterrupted, and successive recitals and dialects narrated from the Messenger of Allah ⁑ into the script, no diacritical dots or marks were included.
4. Five, seven or eight of these *muṣḥafs* were prepared and sent to the major cities of the time.

---

[31] Al-Aẓami, *The History of the Qurʾānic Text*, 103; Najāḥ, *Mukhtasar al-Tabyīn li-Hijāʾ al-Tanzīl*, 1:141.

[32] Ibn al-Jazarī, *al-Nashr fī al-Qirāʾāt al-ʿAshr*, 1:7; *ʿAqīlah Atrāb*, l. 36-37.

[33] Iẓhār Aḥmad Thānwī, *al-Jawāhir al-Naqiyyah*, 14.

[34] Al-Dānī, *al-Muqniʿ*, 106.

5. The same method was adopted this time that was adopted in Abū Bakr's time and the manuscripts prepared by Abū Bakr ؓ were used.
6. This was compiled under the guidance and leadership of ʿUthmān ؓ and with the consensus of 12,000 *ṣaḥāba* ؓ.

Various Divisions of the Qur'ān

Takhmīs/Taʿshīr تخميس تعشير

Takhmīs literally means to count five or make five and *taʿshīr* means to count ten or make ten. It is reported from the famous *tābiʿī*, Qatādah, that the *ṣaḥāba* ﷺ also used to incorporate the signs for every five and ten verses.[35] The letter خ or the word خمس would be placed after every five verses and the letter ع or the word عشر after every ten verses. These would also be referred to as أخماس (*akhmās*) and أعشار (*aʿshār*) respectively.[36] ʿAllāmah al-Dānī says that in all regions from the time of the *tābiʿīn* till this day, scholars have permitted incorporating dots for letters and diacritical marks for words, and the enumeration of the *sūrahs* and the verses contained in the *sūrahs*, and similarly the signs for every five and ten verses.[37]

It is also reported that this was introduced by the great *tābiʿī* from Baṣrah, Naṣr ibn ʿĀṣim al-Laithī.[38]

The *Ajzā'* of the Qur'ān

Ajzā' أجزاء is the plural of جُزء which means a part/portion. During the time of Ḥajjāj, the Qur'ān was divided into thirty almost equal *ajzā'* based on the number of words apart from *sūrah* al-Fātiḥa. Then each *juz* was divided into four almost equal parts with the words ربع for the first quarter, نصف

---

[35] Al-Suyūṭī, *al-Itqān fī ʿUlūm al-Qur'ān*, 4:184.

[36] Shafī Usmānī, *Maʿārif al-Qur'ān*, 1:33; al-Qāḍī, *Tārīkh al-Muṣḥaf al-Sharīf*, 48.

[37] Al-Dānī, *al-Muḥkam*, 2-3.

[38] Al-Suyūṭī, *al-Itqān fī ʿUlūm al-Qur'ān*, 4:184.

for the halfway point and ثلثة for the third quarter.[39] These words for the first three quarters are only marked in the South Asian prints of the Qurʾān. They are not in the *Madanī* prints.

This was probably based on a longer ḥadīth in which the Messenger of Allah ﷺ mentioned to ʿAbd Allah ibn ʿAmr ibn al-ʿĀṣ to complete the Qurʾān in one month,[40] and that many of the pious predecessors had made that their habit.

The scholars of Egypt and the west would divide the Qurʾān into 60 *aḥzāb* أحزاب. *Aḥzāb* is the plural of حِزْب. Each *ḥizb* would be about half a *juz* and each *ḥizb* would further be divided into four parts called ربع الحزب(1/4 of a *ḥizb*) or *al-maqraʾ* المَقْرَأ. This division of *aḥzāb* has been followed by the current *Madanī* prints of the Holy Qurʾān. It is also reported that this was done to facilitate the completion of the whole Qurʾān in one month in eight *rakaʿāt* of *tahajjud*. These are not found in the South Asian prints.

Ajzāʾ for the sake of Reciting the *Qirāʾāt*

Ibn al-Jazarī writes that in his time, some scholars had divided the Qurʾān into 120 *ajzāʾ* so that each *riwāyah* can be completed in four months. Some scholars had divided the Qurʾān into 240 *ajzāʾ* so that in eight months they could complete all fourteen or twenty *riwāyāt* combined.[41]

Rukūʿāt

This division is found in the South Asian prints of the Holy Qurʾān and not in the *Madanī* prints. Its indicator is the letter ع with three numbers; one

[39] Raḥīm Bakhsh Pānīpatī, *al-Khaṭṭ al-ʿUthmānī fī al-Rasm al-Qurʾānī*, 31-32.

[40] Tirmidhī, 2946.

[41] Ibn al-Jazarī, *al-Nashr fī al-Qirāʾāt Al-ʿAshr*, 2:97.

on top that indicates the number of the current *rukūʿ* in the *sūrah*, one number underneath that indicates the number of the current *rukūʿ* in the *juz* and one number in the middle that indicates the number of verses in that *rukūʿ*.

This was introduced mostly by the *Ḥanafī* scholars of *Mā Warāʾ al-Nahr*[42] around the year 300 AH.[43] They saw that people were following the *taʿshīr* (ten verses) signs for each *rakʿah* of *tarāwīḥ*, thus completing the Qurʾān in thirty days i.e., 10 x 20 x 30 = 6,000 verses. However, on many occasions, the meaning of the topic would be left incomplete in each *rakʿah*. So, in order to facilitate that each *rakʿah* consists of a full topic, they devised the system of *rukūʿ* in terms of the completeness of a topic or meaning. In addition to that, they intended that the Qurʾān be completed on the 27th of Ramadan. Hence, they placed 540 *rukūʿāt*[44] at those places where the majority of the time, the topic or meaning is complete and so that the Qurʾān could be completed on the 27th of Ramadan.[45] Another point that was intended is that every *rukūʿ* must consist of sufficient verses through which the obligatory amount of recitation for a *rakʿah* may be fulfilled.[46] Some latter-day scholars have mentioned 558 *rukūʿāt*.[47]

---

42 Refers to Transoxania, which roughly corresponds to present day Central Asia. Historically, this was the land that was east of the Oxus River and west of the Jaxartes River. Britannica, T. Editors of Encyclopaedia. "Transoxania." *Encyclopedia Britannica*, November 4, 2016. https://www.britannica.com/place/Transoxania.

43 Sarakhsī, *al-Mabsūṭ*, 2:146; Sindī, "*Muṣṭalaḥ al-Rukūʿ fī al-Maṣāḥif*," 39.

44 20 units of prayer X 27 nights=540.

45 *Al-Fatāwā al-Hindiyyah*, 1:130.

46 Raḥīm Bakhsh Pānīpatī, *al-Khaṭṭ al-ʿUthmānī fī al-Rasm al-Qurʾānī*, 34-35.

47 This is the division that is used in contemporary *maṣāḥif*. This would not result in a *khatam* on the night of the 27th if only one *rukūʿ* is read in each *rakʿah*. However, one should keep in mind that the *rukūʿāt* in *juz ʿamma* are extremely short, and the reciter can easily read more than one in each *rakʿah*.

A Division of the *Sūwar* Based on Length

Scholars have divided the *sūrahs* of the Qurʾān in terms of their length into the following four categories:[48]

Category Name	Number of Sūrahs	Sūrahs
al-Ṭiwāl (long ones) with more that 100 *āyāt*	8	Al-Baqarah to al-Barāʾah: 2-9.
al-Miʾūn: *Sūrahs* with approximately 100 *āyāt*	26	Yūnus to Fāṭir: 10-35.
al-Mathānī: Sūrahs with less than 100 *āyāt*	14	Yāsīn to al-Ḥujurāt: 36-49.
al-Mufaṣṣal: the last section of the Qurʾān	65	Qāf to al-Nās: 50-114.

Famī bi-Shawq

Famī bi-Shawq فمى بشوق is a division of the Qurʾān into seven *manāzil* منازل (plural of مَنْزِل). This is also based on the aforementioned longer ḥadīth wherein ʿAbd Allah ibn ʿAmr ibn al-ʿĀṣ ﷺ mentions that he is capable of reading more than one completion of the Qurʾān in one month, upon which the Messenger of Allah ﷺ permitted him to recite the Qurʾān in one week.[49] The division is also mentioned in another *ḥadīth* of Abū Dāwūd and

---

[48] Al-Zarkashī, *Al-Burhān fī ʿUlūm al-Qurʾān*, 1:244-245.

[49] Muslim, 1159.

Ibn Mājah wherein it is explicitly mentioned that the *ṣaḥābah* ﷺ used to divide the Qur'ān into seven parts:[50] one for each day of the week. The following chart shows the division:

Manzil Number	Number of Sūrahs	Sūrahs
1	4	Al-Fātiḥa to al-Nisā'
2	5	Al-Mā'idah to al-Barā'ah
3	7	Yūnus to al-Naḥl
4	9	Al-Isrā' or Banū Isrā'īl to al-Furqān
5	11	Al-Shuʿarā' to Yāsīn
6	13	Al-Ṣāffāt to al-Ḥujurāt
7	65	Qāf to al-Nās

Famī bi-Shawq فمى بشوق is an acronym that was introduced in the time of Ḥajjāj as a mnemonic, with each letter standing for the *sūrah* that the *manzil* begins with:[51]

ف for al-Fātiḥa
م for al-Mā'idah
ي for Yūnus
ب for Banū Isrā'īl
ش for al-Shuʿarā'
و for Wa al-Ṣāffāt
ق for Qāf

According to another slight variance, the second *manzil* begins with al-Nisā'. Thus, the acronym would be فني بشوق.

[50] Al-Zarkashī, *al-Burhān fī Ulūm al-Qur'ān*, 1:247; Abū Dāwūd, 1393; Ibn Mājah 1345.
[51] Raḥīm Bakhsh Pānīpatī, *al-Khaṭṭ al-ʿUthmānī fī al-Rasm al-Qur'ānī*, 32-33.

The *Manāzil* of *Aḥzāb*

This is another division of the Qurʾān into seven parts slightly different from the above. Its acronym is فأيط عزو.

ف for al-Fātiḥa
أ for al-Anʿām
ي for Yūnus
ط for Ṭāhā
ع for al-ʿAnkabūt
ز for al-Zumar
و for al-Wāqiʿah

It is reported that ʿUthmān, Zaid, Ubai ibn Kaʿb and Ibn Masʿūd ﷺ would complete a Qurʾān recitation beginning from Friday[52] and completing on Thursday.[53]

It is reported from Ibn ʿAbbās ﷺ that whoever follows suit will have his *duʿāʾ's* accepted.[54]

---

[52] Meaning the night before the day of Friday, as Islamically, Friday begins after Maghreb on Thursday.

[53] Al-Nawawī, *al-Tibyān*, 46; Shafī Usmānī, *Maʿārif al-Qurʾān*, 1:32; Raḥīm Bakhsh Pānīpatī, *al-Khaṭṭ al-ʿUthmānī fī al-Rasm al-Qurʾānī*, 33; al-Ghazālī, *Iḥyā ʿUlūm al-Dīn*, 1:656-657. Thursday here refers to Wednesday night, as the Islamic day begins after Maghreb.

[54] Raḥīm Bakhsh Pānīpatī, *al-Khaṭṭ al-ʿUthmānī fī al-Rasm al-Qurʾānī*, 33.

The Importance of Rasm al-Khaṭṭ

Scholars of *qirā'āt* have stated the following three conditions for determining the validity of a particular *qirā'ah.*[55]

1. The *qirā'ah* must be in accordance with one of the *maṣāḥif* (sing: *muṣḥaf*) prepared by the *Ṣaḥāba* ﷽ under the supervision of the *Khalīfa* ʿUthmān ؓ and sent to various parts of the Islamic world at the time. These were five according to one opinion, seven according to another and eight according to another. These are known as *Maṣāḥif ʿUthmāniyyah* (sing: *Muṣḥaf* ʿUthmāni).
2. The *qirā'ah* must be in accordance to the well-known grammatical principles of *naḥw* (Arabic syntax) and *ṣarf* (Arabic verb conjugation).
3. The transmission must be *mutawātir.*

Definitions

Rasm رسم literally signifies: drawing, sketch, trace, graph, picture, outline, pattern, mark, note, design, regulation, form, rate.

Khaṭṭ خط literally means to write. It can also refer to a line. Synonymous words include *kitābah* الكتابة and *imlā'* الإملاء.

Khaṭṭ is of two types; 1. قياسي *Qiyāsī* (logical) 2. اصطلاحي *Iṣṭilāḥī* (technical)

1. *Khaṭṭ Qiyāsī*: In Arabic academia, it refers to writing a word with its letters the way it is pronounced in the state of *waṣl* and *waqf* i.e., the spelling is exactly according to how the word is pronounced. About 95% of the *rasm* of the Arabic language is *qiyāsī*. There are very few

[55] Ibn al-Jazarī, *al-Nashr fī al-Qirā'āt al-ʿAshr*, 1:9.

exceptions. However, in terms of the *rasm* of the Qurʾān, approximately 80% is *qiyāsī*, the other 20% is *iṣṭilāḥī. Khaṭṭ Qiyāsī* is also known as *rasm imlāʾī* الرسم الإملائي (script according to dictation) or الرسم العادي (script according to what is habitual).

2. *Khaṭṭ Iṣṭilāḥī*: Where the *rasm* (spelling) of the word does not conform to the word or pronunciation. This is the main focus and subject matter in the science of *Rasm al-Khaṭṭ*. Other synonymous terms include:
    - *Rasm al-Muṣḥaf* رسم المصحف
    - *Rasm ʿUthmānī* الرسم العثماني
    - *Khaṭṭ ʿUthmānī* الخط العثماني
    - *Rasm Qurʾānī* الرسم القرآني
    - *Khaṭṭ Qurʾānī* الخط القرآني

Rasm al-Khaṭṭ رسم الخط refers to writing the words of the Qurʾān strictly in accordance to how their spelling was agreed upon by the *Ṣaḥāba* ﷺ and written in the *maṣāḥif* prepared under the guidance of ʿUthmān ﷺ.

Examples of words written in *Rasm al-Khaṭṭ*:

العلمين الرحمن الصلحت نَبَايْ

The same words written in regular Arabic *Khaṭṭ*:

العالمين الرحمان الصالحات نَبَإِ

The word *Khaṭṭ* is also used to refer to the calligraphic style of Arabic writing. Thus, from this perspective, it is permissible to change the *Khaṭṭ* of the Qurʾān, but it is impermissible to change the *Rasm al-Khaṭṭ* of the Qurʾān. For example, while writing the Qurʾān or quoting the above words as part of the Qurʾān, it is permissible to write them in the following or any other font:

العلمين الرحمن الصلحت هؤلاء نَبَائِ

العلمين الرحمن الصلحت هؤلاء نَبَائ

العلمين الرحمن الصلحت هؤلاء نَبَائِ

العلمين الرحمن الصلحت هؤلاء نَبَائِ

However, it is impermissible to write the same words as:

العالمين الرحمان الصالحات هاأُلاء نَبَإِ

Ḍabṭ **ضبط** refers to the usage of diacritical marks to aid pronunciation of letters and words. This is sometimes included in the science of *rasm al-khaṭṭ*. Thus, we say the science of *rasm al-khaṭṭ* and *al-ḍabṭ* and at times when studied as a separate science, the science of *ḍabṭ*.

Subject Matter

The science of *ḍabṭ* deals mainly with how to write the following five diacritical marks:

1. *Ḥarakāt*: *fatḥa*, *ḍammah*, *kasrah*
2. *Sukūn*
3. *Shaddah*
4. *Madd*
5. *Hamza*

Tashkīl تشكيل is a synonymous term with *ḍabṭ*. *Shakl* شَكْل refers to the diacritical marks. *Ashkāl* أشكال is its plural.

Status

The *rasm al-khaṭṭ* of the Qurʾān is an issue based on *tawqīf* توقيف i.e., it was dictated by the Messenger of Allah ﷺ according to how it is preserved in the *Lawḥ Maḥfūẓ* اللوح المحفوظ and inspired to him by Allah *Taʿālā*. There is no scope for logic or opinions in this regard. There is a famous statement of the scholars:

خطان لايقاسان خط القوافي و خط القرأن

There are two types of *Khaṭṭ* that have no scope for logic; The *Khaṭṭ* of *qawāfī* (Arabic poetry) and the *Rasm al-Khaṭṭ* of the Qurʾān.[56]

ʿAllāmah Burhan al-Dīn Abū Isḥāq Ibrāhim ibn ʿUmar al-Jaʿbarī (d. 732 AH) states, "The *rasm al-khaṭṭ* of the Qurʾān is *tawqīfī* and this is the opinion of the scholars of the four schools of thought."[57] A vast majority of the scholars deem it impermissible to write the Qurʾān contrary to *rasm al-khaṭṭ*. Scholars maintain that just like the Qurʾān comprises the words and meanings, and is a miracle from both perspectives, it is also a miracle in terms of its script. Thus, the need arises to study *rasm al-khaṭṭ*.[58]

Mullā ʿAlī al-Qārī writes in one of his works that the Messenger of Allah ﷺ said to one of his scribes Muʿāwiyah ؓ, "Keep the mouth of the ink bottle as wide as possible so that the pen can be easily inserted, keep the cut at the end of the pen slanted, enlarge the *bāʾ* of 'bismi-Allah' and write the teeth (small protruding lines) of the *sīn* with clarity, do not ruin the eye of

---

[56] Nadhr Muḥammad, *Tashīl al-Bayān* translation and foreword by Abū al-Ḥasan Aʿẓamī, 10.

[57] Al-Jaʿbarī, *Jamīlah al-Arbāb al-Marāṣid*, 380.

[58] Nadhr Muḥammad, *Tashīl al-Bayān* translation and foreword by Abū al-Ḥasan Aʿẓamī, 8.

the letter *mīm*, write the word Allah beautifully, enlarge the *nūn* of al-Raḥmān and write al-Raḥīm with precision."[59]

[59] Ibid., 11. Mullā ʿAlī al-Qārī, *Sharḥ al-Shifā lil-Qāḍī ʿIyād*, 1:728.

Arabic Khaṭṭ Throughout History

Arabic has been written in many calligraphic styles throughout history:[60]

1. Muʿqilī معقلي also known as *musnad*. It is said that this was taught to Idrīs ﷺ.

2. Qīrāmūzī قيراموزي

In Makkah al-Mukarramah, the Qurʾān was first written with this Khaṭṭ.

3. Ḥīrī حِيري

In Madīnah al-Munawwarah, the Qurʾān was written with this *khaṭṭ*. As ransom, those prisoners from the Battle of Badr who knew how to write were ordered to teach ten *Ṣaḥābah* ﷺ each. These prisoners being from Ḥīrā were well versed in the Ḥīrī *khaṭṭ*. This became the dominant *khaṭṭ* for the writing of the Qurʾān and this was used in the time of Abū Bakr ﷺ when the Qurʾān was compiled into book form, and this was the same *khaṭṭ* that was used to write the Uthmānī Maṣāḥif.[61] This *khaṭṭ* later on became known as *al-Khaṭṭ al-Ḥijāzī.*[62]

---

[60] Nadhr Muḥammad, *Tashīl al-Bayān* translation and foreword by Abū al-Ḥasan Aʿẓamī, 8-9.

[61] Muhammad Idrīs al-ʿĀṣim, *Nafāʾis al-Bayān*, 32-38.

[62] Muhammad Idrīs al-ʿĀṣim, *Nafāʾis al-Bayān*, 30.

4. Kūfī كوفي

As Islam spread, Muslims were introduced to the Kufī *Khaṭṭ*. Thus, in the year 160 AH the Qur'ān was written in the Kūfī *Khaṭṭ*.[63]
After this period, scholars expanded in the science of *Khaṭṭ* and introduced many different styles and fonts. Ibn Muqlah—one of the governors of the Khalīfah Muqtadir bi Allah, introduced six more styles:

1. Naskh نسخ
2. Thuluth ثلث
3. Rayhān ريحان
4. Tawqīʿ توقيع
5. Muḥaqqaq محقق
6. Riqāʿ/ruqʿah/riqʿah رِقاع رُقعة رِقعة

In the year 318 AH the Qur'ān was written in the *Naskh* style for the first time, and this is the *khaṭṭ* predominantly used since then. This is to such an extent that some have stated an *ijmāʿ* on this style to be adopted for the script of the Qur'ān.

Apart from the above, *Nastaʿlīq*, also known as *taʿlīq*, was introduced and adopted by the Persians and Turks. Nowadays, Urdu and Persian are written in *Nastaʿlīq*. *Nastaʿlīq* was used for Turkish until the rise of Mustafa Attaturk who anglicized the Turkish alphabet.

[63] The Kūfī script was very similar to the Ḥirī script as both these cities were in close geographic proximity to each other. Therefore, it is not impossible that the Qur'ān was written in this script before 160 AH as well. al-Azami, *History of the Qur'ānic Text*, 139.

Books on Rasm al-Khaṭṭ

Scholars throughout the history of Islam wrote on this subject. Beginning from the first century we have:

1. Imam ᶜAbd Allah ibn ᶜĀmir al-Shāmī (d. 118 AH), *Ikhtilāf Maṣāḥif al-Shām wa al-Ḥijāz wa al-ᶜIrāq* and *Kitāb fī Maqṭūᶜ al-Qur'ān wa Mawṣūlih.*[64]
2. Yaḥyā ibn al-Ḥārith al-Dhamārī (d. 145 AH): He is the student of Ibn ᶜĀmir al-Shāmī. He wrote *Kitāb fī Hijā' al-Maṣāḥif.*[65]
3. Imam Ḥamzah ibn Ḥabīb al-Zayyāt al-Kūfī (d. 156 AH), *Kitāb fī Maqṭūᶜ al-Qur'ān wa Mawṣūlih.*[66]
4. Imam al-Kisā'ī al-Kūfī (d. 189 AH), *Ikhtilāf Maṣāḥif Ahl al-Madīnah wa Ahl al-Kūfa wa Ahl al-Baṣrah* and *Kitāb al-Hijā' & Kitāb Maqṭūᶜ al-Qur'ān wa Mawṣūlih.*[67]
5. Farrā' Yaḥyā ibn Ziyād ibn ᶜAbd Allah ibn Manṣūr Abū Zakariyyā al-Aslamī al-Kūfī (d. 207 AH); He is the famous grammarian of Arabic. He wrote *Ikhtilāf Ahl al-Kūfa wa al-Baṣrah wa al-Shām fī al-Maṣāḥif.*[68]
6. Khalaf ibn Hishām (d. 229 AH), *Kitab fī Ikhtilāf al-Maṣāḥif.*[69]
7. Imam Nāfiᶜ ibn Abī Nuᶜaim al-Madanī (d. 169 AH). He is the most prominent and important source for the narration of *rasm al-khaṭṭ*, especially the *muṣḥaf* of Madīnah. He was born in Madīnah and taught *qirā'āt* for seventy years. The *muṣḥaf* prepared by ᶜUthmān ﷺ for the people of Madinah was with Imam Nāfiᶜ for a

---

[64] Ghānim Qaddūrī al-Ḥamad, *al-Muyassar*, 65; Ibn Nadīm, *Fihrist*, 56-57.

[65] Ibid.

[66] Ibid., 66; Ibn Nadīm, *Fihrist*, 56.

[67] Ibid., 70; Ibn Nadīm, *Fihrist*, 55-56.

[68] Ibn Nadīm, *Fihrist*, 55.

[69] Ibid.; Najāḥ, *Mukhtasar al-Tabyīn li-Hijā' al-Tanzīl*, 1:161.

while. Many of his students wrote books on *rasm al-khaṭṭ* narrating from him.[70] They include:

8. Ghāzī ibn Qais al-Andalusī (d. 199 AH), *Hijā᾽ al-Sunnah.* He is one of the preeminent students of Imam Nāfiᶜ and it was through him that the Qirā᾽ah of Imam Nāfiᶜ reached Spain. He prepared a *muṣḥaf* after proofreading it 13 times with the *muṣḥaf* of Imam Nāfiᶜ and thereafter wrote his book.[71]
9. Qālūn (d. 220 AH) the first *rāwī* of Imam Nāfiᶜ. He wrote his book directly relaying from Imam Nāfiᶜ.[72]
10. Abū ᶜUbaid Qāsim ibn Sallām (d. 224 AH), *Faḍā᾽il al-Qur᾽ān wa Maᶜālimuh wa Ādābuh.* There is one chapter in this dealing specifically with *rasm al-khaṭṭ.* He has written about almost every single science of the Sharī᾽ah. [73] He has eight well-known books on the sciences of the Qur᾽ān. His books on *qirā᾽āt* and *tajwīd* are considered to be one of the first.[74]
11. Abū al-Mundhir Naṣīr ibn Yūsuf al-Naḥwī (d. 240 AH) was one of the students of Imam al-Kisā᾽ī. After Imam Nāfiᶜ and Abū ᶜUbaid Qāsim ibn Sallām, he is considered an authority in the science of *rasm al-khaṭṭ.* He wrote a book titled *Rasm al-Maṣāḥif.*[75]

---

[70] Ghānim Qaddūrī al-Ḥamad, *al-Muyassar*, 67-68.

[71] Ghānim Qaddūrī al-Ḥamad, *al-Muyassar*, 68; Najāḥ, *Mukhtasar al-Tabyīn li-Hijā᾽ al-Tanzīl*, 1:159.

[72] Najāḥ, *Mukhtasar al-Tabyīn li-Hijā᾽ al-Tanzīl*, 1:159.

[73] Ibn al-Jazarī, *Ghayah al-Nihāyah*, 2:18.

[74] In the early centuries of Islam, *tajwīd* and *qirā᾽āt* were not distinctly different sciences. Therefore, the great Imam may have mentioned some topics in his works that are now considered topics of *tajwīd*. However, no known complete works on *tajwīd* are assigned to him. Ibn al-Jazarī considers Imam Abū ᶜUbaid to be one of the first who wrote on *qirā᾽āt*. Ibn al-Jazarī, *al-Nashr*, 1:33-34.

[75] Ibn al-Jazarī, *Ghayah al-Nihāyah*, 2:297.

12. Muḥammad ʿĪsa al-Taymī al-Asbahānī (d. 253 AH) was the student of Naṣīr ibn Yūsuf. [He wrote a book on the *rasm* of the Qurʾān,][76] *Hijāʾ al-Maṣāḥif*.[77]

[76] Ibn al-Jazarī, *Ghayah al-Nihāyah*, 2:197.

[77] Najāḥ, *Mukhtasar al-Tabyīn li-Hijāʾ al-Tanzīl*, 1:168.

Principles of Rasm al-Khaṭṭ

This science can be divided into two main parts:

1. *Uṣūl* – General principles that are generally applicable throughout the Qur'ān
2. *Furūsh* – Specific cases that apply to specific words only

The following are the main sources for this science:

1. *Maṣāḥif ʿUthmāniyyah* – Their *rasm* is exactly how the Qur'ān was written during the time of the Messenger of Allah ﷺ. These were prepared under the guidance of ʿUthmān ؓ by Zaid, Ibn ʿAbbās, Ubay ibn Kaʿb, Abd al-Raḥmān ibn al-Ḥārith ibn Hishām, Saʿīd ibn al-ʿĀṣ and ʿAbd Allah ibn Zubair ؓ.[78]
2. Imam Nāfiʿ and the Madanī *Muṣḥaf* – Imam Nāfiʿ narrates the Madanī *rasm* from the *Muṣḥaf* that was prepared for the people of Madīna under the guidance of ʿUthmān ؓ.[79] Whenever Imam Nāfiʿ is mentioned, the Madanī *Muṣḥaf* will be meant and whenever the Madanī *Muṣḥaf* is mentioned, the narration of Imam Nāfiʿ [from it] will be meant.
3. Imam Abū ʿUbaid Qāsim ibn Sallām and the Imam *Muṣḥaf* – Abū ʿUbaid Qāsim ibn Sallām narrates *rasm* from the Imam *Muṣḥaf* i.e., the *Muṣḥaf* that was prepared under the guidance of ʿUthmān ؓ and he had kept it for himself.[80] Whenever Imam Abū ʿUbaid Qāsim ibn Sallām's narration is mentioned, the Imam *Muṣḥaf* will be

[78] Fatḥ Panīpatī, *Ashal al-Mawārid*, 33-34; Najāḥ, *Mukhtasar al-Tabyīn li-Hijā' al-Tanzīl*, 1:138; Ghānim Qaddūrī al-Ḥamad, *al-Muyassar*, 37.

[79] Fatḥ Panīpatī, *Ashal al-Mawārid*, 41.

[80] Ibid.

meant, and whenever the Imam *Muṣḥaf* is mentioned, the narration of Imam Abū ʿUbaid Qāsim ibn Sallām will be meant.

4. Makkī *Muṣḥaf* – The *Muṣḥaf* that was prepared likewise for the people of Makkah.
5. Kūfī *Muṣḥaf* – The *Muṣḥaf* that was prepared likewise for the people of Kūfa.
6. Baṣrī *Muṣḥaf* – The *Muṣḥaf* that was prepared likewise for the people of Baṣrah.
7. ʿIraqī *Muṣḥaf* – Both the Kufī and Basrī *Muṣḥafs* are referred to as the ʿIraqī *Muṣḥafs*.
8. Shāmī *Muṣḥaf* – The *Muṣḥaf* that was prepared likewise for the people of Shām.
9. Baḥrainī *Muṣḥaf* - The *Muṣḥaf* that was prepared likewise for the people of Baḥrain.
10. Yemenī *Muṣḥaf* - The *Muṣḥaf* that was prepared likewise for the people of Yemen.

However, the *Muṣḥafs* of Baḥrain and Yemen are not used as references in this science.

There are five main causes of differences between *khaṭṭ* and *rasm al-khaṭṭ*:

1. *Ḥadhf* حذف dropping of a letter
2. *Ziyādah* زيادة adding a letter
3. *Ibdāl* إبدال transforming a letter into a another letter
4. *Faṣl & Waṣl* الفصل والوصل Separating & Adjoining
5. *Hamz* الهمز Pronouncing a *hamza*

Ḥadhf حذف

Dropping of a letter

Ḥadhf in the ʿUthmānī *Maṣāḥif* occurs due to the following causes:

1. To avoid successive identical letters e.g., two or three *alifs* etc.
2. To accommodate the recital of different *riwāyāt.*
3. Due to the fact that normally *waṣl* is intended and done on that word.
4. Due to a reason other than the above.

Ḥadhf to avoid successive identical letters e.g., two or three *alifs* etc.

Examples of *Ḥadhf* of *alif*:

Verse	Print	Sūrah	Word
فَلَمَّا تَرَٰٓءَا ٱلۡجَمۡعَانِ قَالَ أَصۡحَٰبُ مُوسَىٰٓ إِنَّا لَمُدۡرَكُونَ ٦١	Madanī	الشعراء 26:61	تَرَٰٓءَا
فَلَمَّا تَرَاۤءَ الۡجَمۡعٰنِ قَالَ اَصۡحٰبُ مُوۡسٰۤى اِنَّا لَمُدۡرَكُوۡنَ ۚ ٦١	South Asian	الشعراء 26:61	تَرَاۤءَ

Scholars are unanimous that the above word is written with only one *alif* as ترا. The reason for this is that they did not have a separate shape for the letter *hamza*. Thus, it did not form a part of the written word. If they were to add another *alif* to represent the *hamza*, the word would have two successive *alifs*; something that is disliked, to avoid confusion. Thus, it was dropped from the word. The scholars of *ḍabṭ* added the vertical mini *alif* (also known as *alif al-khanjariyyah* or standing *zabar/fatḥa*) after the *rāʾ* to represent the first *alif* and a *hamza* after it to facilitate its correct recital. Based on this convention of *ḍabṭ*, the first *alif* was dropped.

Using a slightly different convention, in the South Asian Print, the *hamza* was added after the *alif* implying that the second *alif* (*hamza*) was dropped. According to the rules of *rasm imlāʾī*, the word would be written as تراءى or تراءا.

Every word that is supposed to have two *alifs* at the beginning is written with one *alif*. This happens when there is a *hamza al-qaṭʿ* at the beginning of a word whether it is the interrogative *hamza* or otherwise, followed by another *hamza al-qaṭʿ* regardless of the *ḥarakah* on it.

There are many such examples in the Qurʾān out of which some are:

Verse	Print	Sūrah	Word
إِنَّ ٱلَّذِينَ كَفَرُواْ سَوَآءٌ عَلَيۡهِمۡ ءَأَنذَرۡتَهُمۡ أَمۡ لَمۡ تُنذِرۡهُمۡ لَا يُؤۡمِنُونَ ٦	Madanī	البقرة 2:6	ءَأَنذَرۡتَهُمۡ
اِنَّ الَّذِيْنَ كَفَرُوْا سَوَآءٌ عَلَيْهِمْ ءَاَنْذَرْتَهُمْ اَمْ لَمْ تُنْذِرْهُمْ لَا يُؤْمِنُوْنَ ٦	South Asian	البقرة 2:6	ءَاَنْذَرْتَهُمْ

Verse	Print	Sūrah	Word
ءَأَنتُمۡ تَخۡلُقُونَهُۥٓ أَمۡ نَحۡنُ ٱلۡخَٰلِقُونَ ٥٩	Madanī	الواقعة 56:59	ءَأَنتُمۡ
ءَاَنْتُمْ تَخْلُقُوْنَهٗۤ اَمْ نَحْنُ الْخٰلِقُوْنَ ٥٩	South Asian	الواقعة 56:59	ءَاَنْتُمْ

However, if the second *hamza* is *hamza* al-*waṣl*, there is a slight difference in the conventions of *ḍabṭ* adopted by the Madanī and South Asian prints of the Qurʾān. The Madanī print will add a *hamza* preceding the second *hamza* and the South Asian print will not add a separate *hamza* as shown in the examples below:

Verse	Print	Sūrah	Word
أَثُمَّ إِذَا مَا وَقَعَ ءَامَنتُم بِهِۦٓۚ ءَآلۡـَٔـٰنَ وَقَدۡ كُنتُم بِهِۦ تَسۡتَعۡجِلُونَ ٥١	Madanī	يونس 10:51	ءَآلۡـَٔـٰنَ
اَثُمَّ اِذَا مَا وَقَعَ اٰمَنْتُمْ بِهٖ ؕ آٰلْئٰنَ وَقَدْ كُنْتُمْ بِهٖ تَسْتَعْجِلُوْنَ ٥١	South Asian	يونس 10:51	آٰلْئٰنَ

The above words according to *rasm imlāʾī* would be written as آلآن.

Verse	Print	Sūrah	Word
قُلۡ أَرَءَيۡتُم مَّآ أَنزَلَ ٱللَّهُ لَكُم مِّن رِّزۡقٖ فَجَعَلۡتُم مِّنۡهُ حَرَامٗا وَحَلَٰلٗا قُلۡ ءَآللَّهُ أَذِنَ لَكُمۡۖ أَمۡ عَلَى ٱللَّهِ تَفۡتَرُونَ ٥٩	Madanī	يونس 10:59	ءَآللَّهُ
قُلْ اَرَءَيْتُمْ مَّآ اَنْزَلَ اللّٰهُ لَكُمْ مِّنْ رِّزْقٍ فَجَعَلْتُمْ مِّنْهُ حَرَامًا وَّحَلٰلًا ؕ قُلْ آٰللّٰهُ اَذِنَ لَكُمْ اَمْ عَلَى اللّٰهِ تَفْتَرُوْنَ ٥٩	South Asian	يونس 10:59	آٰللّٰهُ

Words like اية ادم امن etc. In the *ʿUthmānī* Muṣḥaf, they are written with one *alif* without the *hamza* on top. The scholars of *ḍabṭ* differ as to how to facilitate reading the *hamza* with the long vowel *alif* without adding an *alif* to the script:

1. The Madanī print has a *hamza* before the *alif* i.e., ءَامَنَ ءَادَم ءَاية
2. The South Asian print has a mini *alif* (*alif khanjariyyah*/standing *fatḥa*) on it.

Rasm *imlāʾī* would be آمن آدم آية or أمن أية أدم

The word الأن wherever it comes in the Qurʾān with or without the interrogative *hamza* is written without the *hamza al-qaṭʿ* and *alif* as follows:

Verse	Print	Sūrah	Word
ٱلۡـَٔـٰنَ خَفَّفَ ٱللَّهُ عَنكُمۡ وَعَلِمَ أَنَّ فِيكُمۡ ضَعۡفٗاۚ فَإِن يَكُن مِّنكُم مِّاْئَةٞ صَابِرَةٞ يَغۡلِبُواْ مِاْئَتَيۡنِۚ وَإِن يَكُن مِّنكُمۡ أَلۡفٞ يَغۡلِبُوٓاْ أَلۡفَيۡنِ بِإِذۡنِ ٱللَّهِۗ وَٱللَّهُ مَعَ ٱلصَّٰبِرِينَ ٦٦	Madanī	الأنفال 8:66	ٱلۡـَٔـٰنَ
اَلْـٰٔنَ خَفَّفَ اللّٰهُ عَنْكُمْ وَعَلِمَ اَنَّ فِيْكُمْ ضَعْفًا ؕ فَاِنْ يَّكُنْ مِّنْكُمْ مِّائَةٌ صَابِرَةٌ يَّغْلِبُوْا مِائَتَيْنِ ۚ وَاِنْ يَّكُنْ مِّنْكُمْ اَلْفٌ يَّغْلِبُوْۤا اَلْفَيْنِ بِاِذْنِ اللّٰهِ ؕ وَاللّٰهُ مَعَ الصّٰبِرِيْنَ ٦٦	South Asian	الأنفال 8:66	اَلْـٰٔنَ

According to *rasm imlāʾī*, it should be written as الآن or اللأن

Verse	Print	Sūrah	Word
أَثُمَّ إِذَا مَا وَقَعَ ءَامَنتُم بِهِۦٓۚ ءَآلۡـَٔـٰنَ وَقَدۡ كُنتُم بِهِۦ تَسۡتَعۡجِلُونَ ٥١	Madanī	يونس 10:51	ءَآلۡـَٔـٰنَ
اَثُمَّ اِذَا مَا وَقَعَ اٰمَنْتُمْ بِهٖ ؕ آٰلْـٰٔنَ وَقَدْ كُنْتُمْ بِهٖ تَسْتَعْجِلُوْنَ ٥١	South Asian	يونس 10:51	آٰلْـٰٔنَ

The above words according to the *rasm imlāʾī* would be written as آلآن with *hamza al-qaṭʿ*.

However, regarding the following الأن in Sūrah al-Jinn, some ʿUthmānī *Muṣḥafs* have it written according to *rasm imlāʾī* and some have it written as الـن.[81] Both Madanī and South Asian prints have it written as الأن according *rasm imlāʾī*.

Verse	Print	Sūrah	Word
وَأَنَّا كُنَّا نَقۡعُدُ مِنۡهَا مَقَٰعِدَ لِلسَّمۡعِۖ فَمَن يَسۡتَمِعِ ٱلۡأٓنَ يَجِدۡ لَهُۥ شِهَابٗا رَّصَدٗا ٩	Madanī	الجن 72:9	ٱلۡأٓنَ

[81] Fatḥ Panīpatī, *Ashal al-Mawārid*, 83.

وَأَنَّا كُنَّا نَقْعُدُ مِنْهَا مَقَاعِدَ لِلسَّمْعِ ۖ فَمَن يَسْتَمِعِ الْآنَ يَجِدْ لَهُ شِهَابًا رَّصَدًا ﴿٩﴾	South Asian	الجن 72:9	الْآنَ

Examples of *Ḥadhf* of *Wāw*

Scholars are unanimous on the *ḥadhf* of one *wāw* when two *wāws* come together in one word. This can take two forms:

1. Both are *wāws* in letter form as in:

الغاون داود يستون

According to *rasm imlāʾī* , they would be written as:

الغاوون داوود يستوون

2. The first *wāw* is actually a *hamza* in *wāw* form and the second is the letter *wāw* as in:

الموءدة تُئويهِ يدْرَءون

According to *rasm imlāʾī*, they would be written as:

الموؤودة تُؤْوِيه يدْرَؤون

Examples of *Ḥadhf* of *Yāʾ*:

Scholars are unanimous on the *Ḥadhf* of one *yāʾ* when two *yā's* come together in one word as in:

يُحْي يستَحْي الأميّن رَبّنِيّن النبيّن وَلِيِّ الله

According to *Rasm Imlāʾī* , they would be written as:

يُحْيِي يستَحْيِي الأميّين رَبّنِيّين النبيّين وَلِيِّيَ الله

In the Madanī print a small *yā'* with its bottom cut-off ـے is placed to inform the reader that a *yā'* must be recited here even though it is not written in the *Muṣḥaf* as in:

إِنَّ ٱلَّذِينَ يَكۡفُرُونَ بِـَٔايَٰتِ ٱللَّهِ وَيَقۡتُلُونَ ٱلنَّبِيِّـۧنَ بِغَيۡرِ حَقّٖ وَيَقۡتُلُونَ ٱلَّذِينَ يَأۡمُرُونَ بِٱلۡقِسۡطِ مِنَ ٱلنَّاسِ فَبَشِّرۡهُم بِعَذَابٍ أَلِيمٍ ٢١

If the dropped *yā'* is *mushaddad*, a *shaddah* is also placed on the mini *yā'* as in:

إِنَّ وَلِـِّۧيَ ٱللَّهُ ٱلَّذِي نَزَّلَ ٱلۡكِتَٰبَۖ وَهُوَ يَتَوَلَّى ٱلصَّٰلِحِينَ ١٩٦

In the South Asian print, the printed *yā'* will have a standing *kasrah* underneath it to denote that it needs to be stretched another *ḥarakah* as in,

يُحْيِ يَسْتَحيِ الْاُمِّيّٖنَ رَبّٰنِيّٖنَ النَّبِيّٖنَ وَلِيّٖ اللهُ

Examples of *Ḥadhf* of *Lām*

Scholars are unanimous on the *Ḥadhf* of one *lām* in the word وَٱلَّٰٓـِٔي of Sūrah al-Ṭalāq. According to *Rasm Imlā'ī*, it would be written as اللائي. Similarly, when ألْ precedes the word ليل, one *lām* will be dropped as in اليل. In order to inform the reader that two *lāms* need to be recited, a *shaddah* is placed on top of the *lām*. According to *Rasm Imlā'ī*, it would be written as الليل.

As for the *Ḥadhf* of *lām* in ٱلَّتِي الذي الذان الذَين الذين التي both *Rasm 'Uthmānī* and *Rasm Imlā'ī* agree upon its *Ḥadhf*.

Similarly, both *rasms* agree on writing both *lāms* in other words beginning with *lām* such as:

اللهو اللغو اللؤلؤ

Examples of *Ḥadhf* of *Nūn*

Scholars are unanimous on the *ḥadhf* of one *nūn* in the following place:

Verse	Number	Sūrah	Word
قَالُواْ يَٰٓأَبَانَا مَالَكَ لَا تَأۡمَ۫نَّا عَلَىٰ يُوسُفَ وَإِنَّا لَهُۥ لَنَٰصِحُونَ ﴿١١﴾	12:11	الأنبياء	تَأۡمَ۫نَّا

Scholars have placed a *shaddah* on the *nūn* to indicate the dropped *nūn*. However, it is not to be recited like a normal *mushaddad* letter. While reciting the *nūn* with the *shaddah, ishmām* needs to be made i.e., one needs to gesture toward the *ḍammah* with his lips to indicate the dropped *nūn* has a *ḍammah*. Another method of reciting it is with *ikhtilās* of the *ḍammah* i.e., recite 2/3 of the *ḍammah* only.

Similarly, scholars are unanimous on the *ḥadhf* of *nūn* in the following verse:[82]

Verse	Print	Sūrah	Word
فَٱسۡتَجَبۡنَا لَهُۥ وَنَجَّيۡنَٰهُ مِنَ ٱلۡغَمِّۚ وَكَذَٰلِكَ نُـۨجِي ٱلۡمُؤۡمِنِينَ ﴿٨٨﴾	Madanī	الأنبياء 21:88	نُـۨجِي

[82] This word is also written without a *nūn* in Sūrah Yūsuf, *āyah* 110. *ʿAqīlah Atrāb*, l. 83.

فَاسْتَجَبْنَا لَهٗ ۙ وَنَجَّيْنٰهُ مِنَ الْغَمِّ ۭ وَكَذٰلِكَ نُـنْجِي الْمُؤْمِنِيْنَ ﴿٨٨﴾	South Asian		نُـنْجِى

Scholars have placed a mini *nūn* to indicate that an extra *nūn* needs to be pronounced. Since there is also *ikhfā'* taking place, the Madanī print does not place a *sukūn* on the *nūn*, whereas the *sukūn* is placed on the *nūn* in the South Asian print.

Ḥadhf **to Accommodate the Recital of Different *Riwāyāt.***

Examples:

1. The *Maṣāḥif* are unanimous on writing the *hamzah al-waṣl* in the word الأيكة in the following two places in the Qur'ān:

Verse	Number	Sūrah	Word
وَإِن كَانَ أَصۡحَٰبُ ٱلۡأَيۡكَةِ لَظَٰلِمِينَ ﴿٧٨﴾	15: 78	الحجر	ٱلۡأَيۡكَةِ
وَّاَصْحٰبُ الْاَيْكَةِ وَقَوْمُ تُبَّعٍ ۭ كُلٌّ كَذَّبَ الرُّسُلَ فَحَقَّ وَعِيْدِ ﴿١٣﴾	50: 14	ق	الْاَيْكَةِ

As for the same word in the following two places, it has been written without the *hamzah al-waṣl* due to the fact that it was revealed with two *qirā'āt*. One with *hamzah al-waṣl*, and that is the *qirā'ah* of Abū ʿAmr, ʿĀṣim, Ḥamza and al-Kisā'ī i.e., ٱلۡأَيۡكَةِ, and the other without *hamzah al-waṣl* and without the following *hamzah al-qatʿ maftūḥah* and with a *fatḥah* at the end of the word.

This is the *qirā'ah* of Nāfiᶜ, Ibn Kathīr, Ibn ᶜĀmir and Abū Jaᶜfar, لَيْكَةَ.[83]

Verse	Number	Sūrah	Word
كَذَّبَ أَصۡحَٰبُ لۡـَٔيۡكَةِ ٱلۡمُرۡسَلِينَ ١٧٦	26: 176	الشعراء	لۡـَٔيۡكَةِ
وَثَمُودُ وَقَوۡمُ لُوطٖ وَأَصۡحَٰبُ لۡـَٔيۡكَةِۚ أُوْلَٰٓئِكَ ٱلۡأَحۡزَابُ ١٣	38: 13	ص	لۡـَٔيۡكَةِ

2. The *Maṣāḥif* are unanimous on the *ḥadhf* of the *yā'* in the following word of the following verse:

Verse	Print	Sūrah	Word
فَلَمَّا جَآءَ سُلَيۡمَٰنَ قَالَ أَتُمِدُّونَنِ بِمَالٖ فَمَآ ءَاتَىٰنِۦَ ٱللَّهُ خَيۡرٞ مِّمَّآ ءَاتَىٰكُمۚ بَلۡ أَنتُم بِهَدِيَّتِكُمۡ تَفۡرَحُونَ ٣٦	Madanī	النمل 27:36	ءَاتَىٰنِۦَ
فَلَمَّا جَآءَ سُلَيۡمٰنَ قَالَ اَتُمِدُّوۡنَنِ بِمَالٍ فَمَاۤ اٰتٰىنَِۦ اللّٰهُ خَيۡرٌ مِّمَّاۤ اٰتٰىكُمۡ بَلۡ اَنۡتُمۡ بِهَدِيَّتِكُمۡ تَفۡرَحُوۡنَ ٣٦	South Asian		ءَاتَىٰنِۦَ

This is to accommodate the differences in the *qirā'āt*. According to the *riwāyah* of Ḥafṣ, the *yā'* will be recited with a *fatḥah* during *waṣl* and during *waqf* both with *yā'* and without *yā'* are reported.[84] The other *qirā'ah* is to recite the word without the *yā'* in both *waṣl* and *waqf*.[85]

3. The *Maṣāḥif* are unanimous on the writing of ال separated from ياسين in the following verse:

---

[83] *Ḥirz al-Amānī wa Wajh al-Tahānī*, l. 928.

[84] Making *waqf* on this word with or without the *yā'* (*ḥadhf* or *ithbāt*) are narrated for Ḥafṣ from the *ṭarīq* of *al-Shāṭibiyyah*.

[85] *Ḥirz al-Amānī wa Wajh al-Tahānī*, l. 429.

Verse	Print	Sūrah	Word
سَلَٰمٌ عَلَىٰٓ إِلۡ يَاسِينَ ١٣٠	Madanī	الصافات 37: 130	إِلۡ يَاسِينَ
سَلٰمٌ عَلٰٓى اِلۡ يَاسِيۡنَ ١٣٠	South Asian		اِلۡ يَاسِيۡنَ

The *qirā'ah* of Nāfi', Ibn 'Āmir and Ya'qūb is آلِ يَاسِيۡنَ (Āli Yāsīn, the family of Yāsīn). The *qirā'ah* of the rest is as above.[86]

The same is the case for all those words that have been revealed with two variances: one with *alif* and the other without. For example:

واعدنا/وعدنا مالك/ملك

Instead of a complete *alif*, a mini *alif* or *alif al-khanjariyyah* is placed to indicate the recitation of *alif*.

Ḥadhf Due to the Fact that Normally *Waṣl* is intended and Done on that Word.

In this case, the scholars of *ḍabṭ* will not place any diacritical mark or letter to indicate the omitted letter.

Examples of Omitting *Alif*

The *alif* has been omitted from the word أيُّها in the following three places:

Verse	Number	Sūrah	Word
وَتُوبُوٓاْ إِلَى ٱللَّهِ جَمِيعًا أَيُّهَ ٱلۡمُؤۡمِنُونَ لَعَلَّكُمۡ تُفۡلِحُونَ ٣١	24: 31	النور	أَيُّهَ

[86] *Ḥirz al-Amānī wa Wajh al-Tahānī*, l. 999-1000; *al-Durrah al-Muḍī'ah*, l. 195.

وَقَالُواْ يَٰٓأَيُّهَ ٱلسَّاحِرُ ٱدۡعُ لَنَا رَبَّكَ بِمَا عَهِدَ عِندَكَ إِنَّنَا لَمُهۡتَدُونَ ﴿٤٩﴾	43: 49	الزخرف	يَٰٓأَيُّهَ
سَنَفۡرُغُ لَكُمۡ أَيُّهَ ٱلثَّقَلَانِ ﴿٣١﴾	55: 31	الرحمن	أَيُّهَ

Examples of Omitting *Wāw*

The *wāw* has been omitted from the following four verbs in the nominative case (*raf*ʿ) in the following verses:

Verse	Number	Sūrah	Word
وَيَدۡعُ ٱلۡإِنسَٰنُ بِٱلشَّرِّ دُعَآءَهُۥ بِٱلۡخَيۡرِۖ وَكَانَ ٱلۡإِنسَٰنُ عَجُولًا ﴿١١﴾	17: 11	الإسراء	يَدۡعُ
أَمۡ يَقُولُونَ ٱفۡتَرَىٰ عَلَى ٱللَّهِ كَذِبًاۖ فَإِن يَشَإِ ٱللَّهُ يَخۡتِمۡ عَلَىٰ قَلۡبِكَۗ وَيَمۡحُ ٱللَّهُ ٱلۡبَٰطِلَ وَيُحِقُّ ٱلۡحَقَّ بِكَلِمَٰتِهِۦٓۚ إِنَّهُۥ عَلِيمُۢ بِذَاتِ ٱلصُّدُورِ ﴿٢٤﴾	42: 24	الشورى	يَمۡحُ
فَتَوَلَّ عَنۡهُمۡۘ يَوۡمَ يَدۡعُ ٱلدَّاعِ إِلَىٰ شَيۡءٖ نُّكُرٍ ﴿٦﴾	54: 6	القمر	يَدۡعُ
سَنَدۡعُ ٱلزَّبَانِيَةَ ﴿١٨﴾	96: 18	العلق	سَنَدۡعُ

Similarly, the *wāw* has been omitted from the following word in the following *āyah*:

Verse	Number	Sūrah	Word
إِن تَتُوبَآ إِلَى ٱللَّهِ فَقَدۡ صَغَتۡ قُلُوبُكُمَاۖ وَإِن تَظَٰهَرَا عَلَيۡهِ فَإِنَّ ٱللَّهَ هُوَ مَوۡلَىٰهُ وَجِبۡرِيلُ وَصَٰلِحُ ٱلۡمُؤۡمِنِينَۖ وَٱلۡمَلَٰٓئِكَةُ بَعۡدَ ذَٰلِكَ ظَهِيرٌ ﴿٤﴾	66:4	التحريم	وَصَٰلِحُ

According to *rasm imlāʾī*, this would be written as صالحو.

Examples of Omitting *Yā*ʾ

Verse	Number	Sūrah	Word
إِلَّا ٱلَّذِينَ تَابُواْ وَأَصْلَحُواْ وَٱعْتَصَمُواْ بِٱللَّهِ وَأَخْلَصُواْ دِينَهُمْ لِلَّهِ فَأُوْلَٰٓئِكَ مَعَ ٱلْمُؤْمِنِينَ وَسَوْفَ يُؤْتِ ٱللَّهُ ٱلْمُؤْمِنِينَ أَجْرًا عَظِيمًا ١٤٦	4: 146	النساء	يُؤْتِ
ٱلْيَوْمَ يَئِسَ ٱلَّذِينَ كَفَرُواْ مِن دِينِكُمْ فَلَا تَخْشَوْهُمْ وَٱخْشَوْنِ	5: 3	المائدة	وَٱخْشَوْنِ
ثُمَّ نُنَجِّي رُسُلَنَا وَٱلَّذِينَ ءَامَنُواْ كَذَٰلِكَ حَقًّا عَلَيْنَا نُنجِ ٱلْمُؤْمِنِينَ ١٠٣	10: 103	يونس	نُنجِ
إِنِّيٓ أَنَا۠ رَبُّكَ فَٱخْلَعْ نَعْلَيْكَ إِنَّكَ بِٱلْوَادِ ٱلْمُقَدَّسِ طُوًى ١٢	20: 12	طه	بِٱلْوَادِ

Ḥadhf Due to a Reason Other than the Above

Omission of the *alif* of *wāw al-jam*ʿ in the following places: The *alif* of *wāw al-jam*ʿ also known as *alif al-faṣl* (*alif* of separation) is the *alif* that is written after the *wāw* that represents the past tense verb being in the third person plural masculine form e.g., قالوا سَجَدوا. This occurs in the words جاءو and باءو wherever they occur in the Qurʾān.[87] Apart from these two words, this occurs in the following four verbs as well:[88]

---

[87] ʿ*Aqīlah Atrāb*, l. 160.

[88] ʿ*Aqīlah Atrāb*, l. 160-161.

Verse	Number	Sūrah	Word
لِّلَّذِينَ يُؤْلُونَ مِن نِّسَآئِهِمْ تَرَبُّصُ أَرْبَعَةِ أَشْهُرٍ فَإِن فَآءُو فَإِنَّ ٱللَّهَ غَفُورٌ رَّحِيمٌ ﴿٢٢٦﴾	2: 226	البقرة	فَآءُو
۞وَقَالَ ٱلَّذِينَ لَا يَرْجُونَ لِقَآءَنَا لَوْلَآ أُنزِلَ عَلَيْنَا ٱلْمَلَٰٓئِكَةُ أَوْ نَرَىٰ رَبَّنَا لَقَدِ ٱسْتَكْبَرُوا۟ فِىٓ أَنفُسِهِمْ وَعَتَوْ عُتُوًّا كَبِيرًا ﴿٢١﴾	25: 21	الفرقان	وَعَتَوْ
وَٱلَّذِينَ سَعَوْ فِىٓ ءَايَٰتِنَا مُعَٰجِزِينَ أُو۟لَٰٓئِكَ لَهُمْ عَذَابٌ مِّن رِّجْزٍ أَلِيمٌ ﴿٥﴾	34: 5	سبإ	سَعَوْ
وَٱلَّذِينَ تَبَوَّءُو ٱلدَّارَ وَٱلْإِيمَٰنَ مِن قَبْلِهِمْ يُحِبُّونَ مَنْ هَاجَرَ إِلَيْهِمْ وَلَا يَجِدُونَ فِى صُدُورِهِمْ حَاجَةً مِّمَّآ أُوتُوا۟ وَيُؤْثِرُونَ عَلَىٰٓ أَنفُسِهِمْ وَلَوْ كَانَ بِهِمْ خَصَاصَةٌ وَمَن يُوقَ شُحَّ نَفْسِهِۦ فَأُو۟لَٰٓئِكَ هُمُ ٱلْمُفْلِحُونَ ﴿٩﴾	59: 9	الحشر	تَبَوَّءُو

Similarly, the *alif* that is normally written after a *wāw aṣli* (root-letter *wāw*) has been omitted from the following word in the following *āyah:*[89]

Verse	Number	Sūrah	Word
فَأُو۟لَٰٓئِكَ عَسَى ٱللَّهُ أَن يَعْفُوَ عَنْهُمْ وَكَانَ ٱللَّهُ عَفُوًّا غَفُورًا ﴿٩٩﴾	4: 99	النساء	يَعْفُوَ

1. *Ḥadhf* of the *alifs* in *jamʿ mudhakkar sālim*, for example:

   العلمين الظلمين خسئين

2. *Ḥadhf* of the *alifs* in *jamʿ muʾannath sālim*, for example:

[89] *ʿAqīlah Atrāb*, l. 161.

مسلمت مؤمنت قنتت تئبت

3. *Ḥadhf* of the *alifs* in *asmāʾ al-ʿadad* أسماء العدد (nouns denoting numbers), for example:

ثلثة ثلثين ثمنية ءالف

According to *rasm imlāʾī*, these words are written with *alif* and sometimes without.

4. *Ḥadhf* of the *alif* of *hāʾ al-tanbīh*, for example:

هذا هؤلاء هأنتم

According to *rasm imlāʾī*, the above words are normally written without *alif.*

5. *Ḥadhf* of the *alif* in *asmāʾ al-ishārah* (demonstrative pronouns), for example,

ذلك كذلك أولئك ذنك

6. *Ḥadhf* of the *alif* in *asmāʾ al-mawṣūlah* (relative pronouns), for example:

ٱلَّٰٓـِٔى ٱلَّٰتِى

According to *rasm imlāʾī*, these words would be written as:

اللائي اللاتي

7. *Ḥadhf* of the *alif* in لكنَّ and لكنْ wherever they occur.
8. *Ḥadhf* of the *alif* in *yāʾ* used for *nidāʾ* (to call someone), for example:

يأيها ينُوح يسماء يأسفى

9. *Ḥadhf* of the medial *alif* in those non-Arab names that have greater than three letters, for example:[90]

إبرهم إسمعيل إسحق هرون عمران

[90] There are some names that are an exception to this rule. *ʿAqīlah Atrāb*, l. 147-149.

Note: In the word Ibrāhīm, the *alif* is omitted throughout the Qurʾān and the *yāʾ* is omitted in *Sūrah* al-Baqarah only. This concurs with the *qirāʾah* of Ibn ʿĀmir: إبراهام.

10. *Ḥadhf* of the *alif* in the word كتاب wherever it occurs except in the following four places:[91]

Verse	Number	Sūrah	Word
وَلَقَدْ أَرْسَلْنَا رُسُلًا مِّن قَبْلِكَ وَجَعَلْنَا لَهُمْ أَزْوَٰجًا وَذُرِّيَّةً وَمَا كَانَ لِرَسُولٍ أَن يَأْتِيَ بِـَٔايَةٍ إِلَّا بِإِذْنِ ٱللَّهِ لِكُلِّ أَجَلٍ كِتَابٌ ۝	13: 38	الرعد	كِتَابٌ
وَمَآ أَهْلَكْنَا مِن قَرْيَةٍ إِلَّا وَلَهَا كِتَابٌ مَّعْلُومٌ ۝	15: 4	الحجر	كِتَابٌ
وَٱتْلُ مَآ أُوحِيَ إِلَيْكَ مِن كِتَابِ رَبِّكَ لَا مُبَدِّلَ لِكَلِمَٰتِهِ وَلَن تَجِدَ مِن دُونِهِ مُلْتَحَدًا ۝	18: 27	الكهف	كِتَابِ
طسٓ تِلْكَ ءَايَٰتُ ٱلْقُرْءَانِ وَكِتَابٍ مُّبِينٍ ۝	27: 1	النمل	كِتَابٌ

11. *Ḥadhf* of the *alif* in the following word of the following *āyah*:[92]

Verse	Number	Sūrah	Word
إِذْ أَنتُم بِٱلْعُدْوَةِ ٱلدُّنْيَا وَهُم بِٱلْعُدْوَةِ ٱلْقُصْوَىٰ وَٱلرَّكْبُ أَسْفَلَ مِنكُمْ وَلَوْ تَوَاعَدتُّمْ لَٱخْتَلَفْتُمْ فِى ٱلْمِيعَٰدِ وَلَٰكِن لِّيَقْضِيَ ٱللَّهُ أَمْرًا كَانَ مَفْعُولًا لِّيَهْلِكَ مَنْ هَلَكَ عَن بَيِّنَةٍ وَيَحْيَىٰ مَنْ حَىَّ عَن بَيِّنَةٍ وَإِنَّ ٱللَّهَ لَسَمِيعٌ عَلِيمٌ ۝	8: 42	الأنفال	ٱلْمِيعَٰدِ

In all other places, the *alif* has been written.

---

[91] *ʿAqīlah Atrāb*, l. 143-144.

[92] *ʿAqīlah Atrāb*, l. 141.

13. *Ḥadhf* of the *alif* in the following word in the following places:[93]

Verse	Number	Sūrah	Word
وَإِن تَعْجَبْ فَعَجَبٌ قَوْلُهُمْ أَءِذَا كُنَّا تُرَٰبًا أَءِنَّا لَفِى خَلْقٍ جَدِيدٍ ۗ أُو۟لَـٰٓئِكَ ٱلَّذِينَ كَفَرُوا۟ بِرَبِّهِمْ ۖ وَأُو۟لَـٰٓئِكَ ٱلْأَغْلَـٰلُ فِىٓ أَعْنَاقِهِمْ ۖ وَأُو۟لَـٰٓئِكَ أَصْحَـٰبُ ٱلنَّارِ ۖ هُمْ فِيهَا خَـٰلِدُونَ ﴿٥﴾	13: 5	الرعد	تُرَٰبًا
وَقَالَ ٱلَّذِينَ كَفَرُوٓا۟ أَءِذَا كُنَّا تُرَٰبًا وَءَابَآؤُنَآ أَئِنَّا لَمُخْرَجُونَ ﴿٦٧﴾	27: 67	النمل	تُرَٰبًا
إِنَّآ أَنذَرْنَـٰكُمْ عَذَابًا قَرِيبًا يَوْمَ يَنظُرُ ٱلْمَرْءُ مَا قَدَّمَتْ يَدَاهُ وَيَقُولُ ٱلْكَافِرُ يَـٰلَيْتَنِى كُنتُ تُرَٰبًۢا ﴿٤٠﴾	78: 40	النبأ	تُرَٰبًا

In all other places, the *alif* has been written.

14. *Ḥadhf* of the *yāʾ* after *hamza* and *Ḥadhf* of the *alif* after *lām* in the following word of the following Sūrah:

Verse	Number	Sūrah	Word
إِۦلَـٰفِهِمْ رِحْلَةَ ٱلشِّتَآءِ وَٱلصَّيْفِ ﴿٢﴾	106:2	قريش	إِۦلَـٰفِهِم

15. *Ḥadhf* of the *wāw* of *hāʾ al-kināyah* [even] when *ṣilah* needs to be made on the *ḍammah*. *Ṣilah* of the *ḍammah* is done when the letter before [and after] *hāʾ al-kināyah* is *mutaharrik*, for example:

Madanī print: لَهُۥ يَحْفَظُونَهُۥ تُنَبِّـُٔونَهُۥ بَعْضَهُۥ عِندَهُۥ

[93] ʿ*Aqīlah Atrāb*, l. 141.

In the earlier days, they would write the *wāw* in red or another color to distinguish it from the Qurʾān.[94] Then gradually they resorted to writing it the same color but making it smaller as to keep it distinct from the Qurʾān.

South Asian print: مَعَهٗ مِّثْلُهٗ لَهٗ يَحْفَظُوْنَهٗ

According to the *qirāʾah* of Ibn Kathīr, *ṣilah* will always be done on it except when connecting to the next word. This is in the state of *waṣl*. During *waqf*, however, all agree that *ṣilah* will not be made.

16. *Ḥadhf* of the *yāʾ* of *hāʾ al-kināyah* [even] when *ṣilah* needs to be made on the *kasrah*. *Ṣilah* of the *kasrah* is done when the letter before it [and after it] is *mutaḥarrik*, for example:

Madanī print: دُونِهِۦ كَخَلْقِهِۦ بِحَمْدِهِۦ خَلْفِهِۦ رَبِّهِۦ بِهِۦ

In the earlier days, they would write the [*yāʾ*] in red or another color to distinguish it from the Qurʾān.[95] Then gradually they resorted to writing it the same color but making it smaller as to keep it distinct from the Qurʾān.

South Asian print: كَخَلْقِهٖ خِيْفَتِهٖ بِحَمْدِهٖ دُوْنِهٖ بِهٖ رَّبِّهٖ

According to the *qirāʾah* of Ibn Kathīr, *ṣilah* will always be done on it except when connecting to the next word. This is in the state of *waṣl*. During *waqf*, however, all agree that *ṣilah* will not be made.

Other than the above categories, there are other individual words that are written without *alif* but do not fall under any general rule.

---

[94] Al-Dānī, *al-Muḥkam*, 55.

[95] Ibid.

The following are words in the Qurʾān wherein both *Rasm ʿUthmānī* and *Rasm Imlāʾī* are the same:

لكن أولئك ذلك الله إله هذا هذه هؤلاء هذان الرحمن الرحيم الذى التى الذين

Ziyādah الزيادة

Addition of Letters

Ziyādah refers to adding a letter to the word without reciting it. The letters that are added to some words in *rasm* ʿUthmānī are *alif*, *wāw* and *yā*ʾ. In all the following examples, the additional letter will not be recited in *waqf* or in *waṣl*. The scholars of *ḍabt* in the Madanī print have placed a small circle on top of such additional letters. In the South Asian print, such additional letters are left empty without any sign to indicate that it is not to be read.

Addition of *Alif*

1. When the *hamza* is seated on a *wāw* and is at the end of a word, for example:

إن امرؤا   يعبؤا   تفتؤا   بُرَءاؤا   تَظمؤا   يبدؤا   الضعفؤا

2. At the end of the word رِبا whose *wāw* is a root letter and normally would be written as an *alif*. In the Qurʾān, it is written as رِبوا.

3. In the word مِئَة wherever it appears in the Qurʾān. It is written as مِائَة, possibly to distinguish it from مِنه, because at the time dots were not incorporated. In *rasm imlā*ʾī, it is sometimes written with *alif* and sometimes without.

4. In the word شيء in the following *āyah* only:

Verse	Number	Sūrah	Word
وَلَا تَقُولَنَّ لِشَاْىْءٍ إِنِّي فَاعِلٌ ذَٰلِكَ غَدًا ﴿٢٣﴾	18: 23	الكهف	لِشَاْىْءٍ

It is said that this is based on the habit of the Arabs at the time that they would sometimes add an *alif* in order to denote that the previous letter should be read with a *fatḥah.*[96]

1. Addition of *alif* in the following words in their respective *āyāt*:

Verse	Number	Sūrah	Word
وَلَوْ أَنَّ قُرْءَانًا سُيِّرَتْ بِهِ ٱلْجِبَالُ أَوْ قُطِّعَتْ بِهِ ٱلْأَرْضُ أَوْ كُلِّمَ بِهِ ٱلْمَوْتَىٰ ۗ بَل لِّلَّهِ ٱلْأَمْرُ جَمِيعًا ۗ أَفَلَمْ يَا۟يْـَٔسِ ٱلَّذِينَ ءَامَنُوٓا۟ أَن لَّوْ يَشَآءُ ٱللَّهُ لَهَدَى ٱلنَّاسَ جَمِيعًا ۗ وَلَا يَزَالُ ٱلَّذِينَ كَفَرُوا۟ تُصِيبُهُم بِمَا صَنَعُوا۟ قَارِعَةٌ أَوْ تَحُلُّ قَرِيبًا مِّن دَارِهِمْ حَتَّىٰ يَأْتِىَ وَعْدُ ٱللَّهِ ۚ إِنَّ ٱللَّهَ لَا يُخْلِفُ ٱلْمِيعَادَ ﴿٣١﴾	13: 31	الرعد	يَا۟يْـَٔسِ
يَٰبَنِىَّ ٱذْهَبُوا۟ فَتَحَسَّسُوا۟ مِن يُوسُفَ وَأَخِيهِ وَلَا تَا۟يْـَٔسُوا۟ مِن رَّوْحِ ٱللَّهِ ۖ إِنَّهُۥ لَا يَا۟يْـَٔسُ مِن رَّوْحِ ٱللَّهِ إِلَّا ٱلْقَوْمُ ٱلْكَٰفِرُونَ ﴿٨٧﴾	12: 87	يوسف	تَا۟يْـَٔسُوا۟ يَا۟يْـَٔسُ
لَوْ خَرَجُوا۟ فِيكُم مَّا زَادُوكُمْ إِلَّا خَبَالًا وَلَأَوْضَعُوا۟ خِلَٰلَكُمْ يَبْغُونَكُمُ ٱلْفِتْنَةَ وَفِيكُمْ سَمَّٰعُونَ لَهُمْ ۗ وَٱللَّهُ عَلِيمٌۢ بِٱلظَّٰلِمِينَ ﴿٤٧﴾	9: 47	البراءة	وَلَأَوْضَعُوا۟ [97]
لَأُعَذِّبَنَّهُۥ عَذَابًا شَدِيدًا أَوْ لَأَا۟ذْبَحَنَّهُۥٓ أَوْ لَيَأْتِيَنِّى بِسُلْطَٰنٍ مُّبِينٍ ﴿٢١﴾	27: 21	النمل	لَأَا۟ذْبَحَنَّهُۥٓ
وَأَشْرَقَتِ ٱلْأَرْضُ بِنُورِ رَبِّهَا وَوُضِعَ ٱلْكِتَٰبُ وَجِا۟ىٓءَ بِٱلنَّبِيِّـۧنَ وَٱلشُّهَدَآءِ وَقُضِىَ بَيْنَهُم بِٱلْحَقِّ وَهُمْ لَا يُظْلَمُونَ ﴿٦٩﴾	39: 69	الزمر	وَجِا۟ىٓءَ
وَجِا۟ىٓءَ يَوْمَئِذٍۭ بِجَهَنَّمَ ۚ يَوْمَئِذٍ يَتَذَكَّرُ ٱلْإِنسَٰنُ وَأَنَّىٰ لَهُ ٱلذِّكْرَىٰ ﴿٢٣﴾	89: 23	الفجر	وَجِا۟ىٓءَ

[96] Ghānim Qaddūrī al-Ḥamad, *al-Muyassar*, 220.

[97] This word can be written with or without an extra *alif*. Al-Dānī, *al-Muqni*ʿ, 85. In the Madinah printed *muṣḥaf* it is written without an extra *alif*, while in the South Asian and South African printed *muṣāḥif* it is written with an extra *alif*, as لَأَاوْضَعُوا.

2. Addition of *alif* in the words ابن and ابنت wherever they appear. In *rasm imlāʾī* they are normally written without the *alif* when connected to the previous word as in بن and بنت.

3. In the following two places, the *nūn sākinah*[98] has been written as an *alif* and the scholars [of *ḍabṭ*] placed the *fatḥatain* (double *fatḥa*) *tanwīn* to facilitate the pronunciation of *nūn sākinah*:

Verse	Number	Sūrah	Word
قَالَتْ فَذَٰلِكُنَّ ٱلَّذِى لُمْتُنَّنِى فِيهِ ۖ وَلَقَدْ رَٰوَدتُّهُۥ عَن نَّفْسِهِۦ فَٱسْتَعْصَمَ ۖ وَلَئِن لَّمْ يَفْعَلْ مَآ ءَامُرُهُۥ لَيُسْجَنَنَّ وَلَيَكُونًا مِّنَ ٱلصَّٰغِرِينَ ﴿٣٢﴾	12: 32	يوسف	وَلَيَكُونًا
كَلَّا لَئِن لَّمْ يَنتَهِ لَنَسْفَعًۢا بِٱلنَّاصِيَةِ ﴿١٥﴾	96: 15	العلق	لَنَسْفَعًا

In *rasm imlāʾī*, these words would be written as لَيَكُونَنْ and لَنَسْفَعَنْ.

4. Writing of the *nūn sākinah* in إِذَنْ as an *alif* i.e., إذاً and placing the *tanwīn* in order to facilitate the pronunciation of the *nūn sākinah.*

5. Writing of the *kasratain* (double *kasrah*) *tanwīn* as *nūn sākinah* in the word كَأَيِّن wherever it appears. This word in *rasm imlāʾī* would be written as كَأَيٍّ.

---

[98] This *nūn sākinah* is a *nūn khafīfah* which appears in verbs to add emphasis.

Addition of Wāw

In the Madanī *Muṣḥaf*, a small circle is placed on top of the *wāw* in those places where it is additional and not to be pronounced in *waqf* and *waṣl*. The South Asian prints leave the *wāw* empty of diacritical marks to indicate that it is not to be pronounced in *waqf* and *waṣl*.

The *wāw* is additional in the word سَأُوريكم wherever it appears.[99] It is said that the *wāw's* purpose is to indicate that a *ḍammah* needs to be read on the preceding *hamza*.

Rasm ʿUthmānī and *rasm imlāʾī*, both have an additional *wāw* in the following words:

أولى: the plural of ذى, in order to distinguish it from إلى
أولئك: in order to distinguish it from إليك
To maintain consistency, the same ruling is applied to أولوا أولئكم أولاء أولات

Addition of *Yāʾ*

In the Madanī Muṣḥaf, a small circle is placed on top of the *yāʾ* in those places where it is additional and not to be pronounced in *waqf* and *waṣl*. The South Asian prints leave the *yāʾ* empty of diacritical marks to indicate that it is not to be pronounced in *waqf* and *waṣl*.

The following places are where *yāʾ* is additional:

---

99 Al-Dānī, *al-Muqniʿ*, 99. This word occurs twice in the Qurʾān, in Sūrah al-Aʿrāf, *āyah* 145 and Sūrah al-Anbiyāʾ, *āyah* 37.

Verse	Number	Sūrah	Word
وَلَقَدۡ كُذِّبَتۡ رُسُلٞ مِّن قَبۡلِكَ فَصَبَرُواْ عَلَىٰ مَا كُذِّبُواْ وَأُوذُواْ حَتَّىٰٓ أَتَىٰهُمۡ نَصۡرُنَاۚ وَلَا مُبَدِّلَ لِكَلِمَٰتِ ٱللَّهِۚ وَلَقَدۡ جَآءَكَ مِن نَّبَإِيْ ٱلۡمُرۡسَلِينَ ٣٤	6: 34	الأنعام	نَّبَإِيْ
فَٱصۡبِرۡ عَلَىٰ مَا يَقُولُونَ وَسَبِّحۡ بِحَمۡدِ رَبِّكَ قَبۡلَ طُلُوعِ ٱلشَّمۡسِ وَقَبۡلَ غُرُوبِهَاۖ وَمِنۡ ءَانَآيِٕ ٱلَّيۡلِ فَسَبِّحۡ وَأَطۡرَافَ ٱلنَّهَارِ لَعَلَّكَ تَرۡضَىٰ ١٣٠	20: 130	طه	ءَانَآيِٕ
وَإِذَا تُتۡلَىٰ عَلَيۡهِمۡ ءَايَاتُنَا بَيِّنَٰتٖ قَالَ ٱلَّذِينَ لَا يَرۡجُونَ لِقَآءَنَا ٱئۡتِ بِقُرۡءَانٍ غَيۡرِ هَٰذَآ أَوۡ بَدِّلۡهُۚ قُلۡ مَا يَكُونُ لِيٓ أَنۡ أُبَدِّلَهُۥ مِن تِلۡقَآيِٕ نَفۡسِيٓۖ إِنۡ أَتَّبِعُ إِلَّا مَا يُوحَىٰٓ إِلَيَّۖ إِنِّيٓ أَخَافُ إِنۡ عَصَيۡتُ رَبِّي عَذَابَ يَوۡمٍ عَظِيمٖ ١٥	10: 15	يونس	تِلۡقَآيِٕ
۞وَمَا كَانَ لِبَشَرٍ أَن يُكَلِّمَهُ ٱللَّهُ إِلَّا وَحۡيًا أَوۡ مِن وَرَآيِٕ حِجَابٍ أَوۡ يُرۡسِلَ رَسُولٗا فَيُوحِيَ بِإِذۡنِهِۦ مَا يَشَآءُۚ إِنَّهُۥ عَلِيٌّ حَكِيمٞ ٥١	42: 51	الشورى	وَرَآيِٕ
۞إِنَّ ٱللَّهَ يَأۡمُرُ بِٱلۡعَدۡلِ وَٱلۡإِحۡسَٰنِ وَإِيتَآيِٕ ذِي ٱلۡقُرۡبَىٰ وَيَنۡهَىٰ عَنِ ٱلۡفَحۡشَآءِ وَٱلۡمُنكَرِ وَٱلۡبَغۡيِۚ يَعِظُكُمۡ لَعَلَّكُمۡ تَذَكَّرُونَ ٩٠	16: 90	النحل	وَإِيتَآيِٕ
أَوَلَمۡ يَتَفَكَّرُواْ فِيٓ أَنفُسِهِمۗ مَّا خَلَقَ ٱللَّهُ ٱلسَّمَٰوَٰتِ وَٱلۡأَرۡضَ وَمَا بَيۡنَهُمَآ إِلَّا بِٱلۡحَقِّ وَأَجَلٖ مُّسَمّٗىۗ وَإِنَّ كَثِيرٗا مِّنَ ٱلنَّاسِ بِلِقَآيِٕ رَبِّهِمۡ لَكَٰفِرُونَ ٨	30: 8	الروم	بِلِقَآيِٕ
وَأَمَّا ٱلَّذِينَ كَفَرُواْ وَكَذَّبُواْ بِـَٔايَٰتِنَا وَلِقَآيِٕ ٱلۡأٓخِرَةِ فَأُوْلَٰٓئِكَ فِي ٱلۡعَذَابِ مُحۡضَرُونَ ١٦	30: 16	الروم	وَلِقَآيِٕ

وَمَا مُحَمَّدٌ إِلَّا رَسُولٌ قَدْ خَلَتْ مِن قَبْلِهِ ٱلرُّسُلُ ۚ أَفَإِيْن مَّاتَ أَوْ قُتِلَ ٱنقَلَبْتُمْ عَلَىٰٓ أَعْقَـٰبِكُمْ ۚ وَمَن يَنقَلِبْ عَلَىٰ عَقِبَيْهِ فَلَن يَضُرَّ ٱللَّهَ شَيْـًٔا ۗ وَسَيَجْزِى ٱللَّهُ ٱلشَّـٰكِرِينَ ١٤٤	3: 144	أل عمران	أَفَإِيْن
وَمَا جَعَلْنَا لِبَشَرٍ مِّن قَبْلِكَ ٱلْخُلْدَ ۖ أَفَإِيْن مِّتَّ فَهُمُ ٱلْخَـٰلِدُونَ ٣٤	21: 34	الأنبياء	أَفَإِيْن
وَٱلسَّمَآءَ بَنَيْنَـٰهَا بِأَيْيْدٍ وَإِنَّا لَمُوسِعُونَ ٤٧	51: 47	الذاريات	بِأَيْيْدٍ
بِأَييِّكُمُ ٱلْمَفْتُونُ ٦	68: 6	القلم	بِأَييِّكُم

2. Similarly wherever the word ملأ is followed by an attached pronoun, an additional *yā*ʾ will be written as in مَلَإِيهم مَلَإِيه.[100] It is said that the *yā*ʾ in the above words has been added to indicate that the preceding *hamza* will be read with a *kasrah*.[101]

---

[100] ʿ*Aqīlah Atrāb*, l. 192.

[101] Ghānim Qaddūrī al-Ḥamad, *al-Muyassar*, 220.

الإبدال Ibdāl

Transformation of Letters

If the transformed letter is in the *rasm* and its pronunciation is according to the *rasm*, the scholars of *ḍabt* will leave it as it is. If the pronunciation is different, the scholars of *ḍabt* will place a diacritical mark to indicate the correct pronunciation.

1. *Ibdāl* of the round *tāʾ al-taʾnīth* ة into the elongated (*mabsūṭah*) *tāʾ* ت, for example:

نِعمت جَنَّت لَعْنَت

This is based on the fact that some tribes actually pronounced the ة as ت in *waṣl* and *waqf*.[102]

2. *Ibdāl* of the *alif* in لَإِنْ into *yāʾ* in لَئِنْ in order to indicate that the *hamza* (originally called *alif*) is to be read with *kasrah*.

3. *Ibdāl* of *alif* to *wāw* in the following four words wherever they appear:

الصلوة الزكوة الحيوة الربوا

And in the following specific words and their respective *āyāt*:

---

102 Mullā ʿAlī al-Qārī, *al-Minaḥ al-Fikriyyah*, 299.

Verse	Number	Sūrah	Word
وَلَا تَطْرُدِ ٱلَّذِينَ يَدْعُونَ رَبَّهُم بِٱلْغَدَوٰةِ وَٱلْعَشِيِّ يُرِيدُونَ وَجْهَهُۥ ۖ مَا عَلَيْكَ مِنْ حِسَابِهِم مِّن شَىْءٍ وَمَا مِنْ حِسَابِكَ عَلَيْهِم مِّن شَىْءٍ فَتَطْرُدَهُمْ فَتَكُونَ مِنَ ٱلظَّٰلِمِينَ ﴿٥٢﴾	6: 52	الأنعام	بِٱلْغَدَوٰةِ
وَٱصْبِرْ نَفْسَكَ مَعَ ٱلَّذِينَ يَدْعُونَ رَبَّهُم بِٱلْغَدَوٰةِ وَٱلْعَشِيِّ يُرِيدُونَ وَجْهَهُۥ ۖ وَلَا تَعْدُ عَيْنَاكَ عَنْهُمْ تُرِيدُ زِينَةَ ٱلْحَيَوٰةِ ٱلدُّنْيَا ۖ وَلَا تُطِعْ مَنْ أَغْفَلْنَا قَلْبَهُۥ عَن ذِكْرِنَا وَٱتَّبَعَ هَوَىٰهُ وَكَانَ أَمْرُهُۥ فُرُطًا ﴿٢٨﴾	18: 28	الكهف	بِٱلْغَدَوٰةِ
۞ ٱللَّهُ نُورُ ٱلسَّمَٰوَٰتِ وَٱلْأَرْضِ ۚ مَثَلُ نُورِهِۦ كَمِشْكَوٰةٍ فِيهَا مِصْبَاحٌ ۖ ٱلْمِصْبَاحُ فِى زُجَاجَةٍ ۖ ٱلزُّجَاجَةُ كَأَنَّهَا كَوْكَبٌ دُرِّىٌّ يُوقَدُ مِن شَجَرَةٍ مُّبَٰرَكَةٍ زَيْتُونَةٍ لَّا شَرْقِيَّةٍ وَلَا غَرْبِيَّةٍ يَكَادُ زَيْتُهَا يُضِىٓءُ وَلَوْ لَمْ تَمْسَسْهُ نَارٌ ۚ نُّورٌ عَلَىٰ نُورٍ ۗ يَهْدِى ٱللَّهُ لِنُورِهِۦ مَن يَشَآءُ ۚ وَيَضْرِبُ ٱللَّهُ ٱلْأَمْثَٰلَ لِلنَّاسِ ۗ وَٱللَّهُ بِكُلِّ شَىْءٍ عَلِيمٌ ﴿٣٥﴾	24: 35	النور	كَمِشْكَوٰةٍ
۞ وَيَٰقَوْمِ مَا لِىٓ أَدْعُوكُمْ إِلَى ٱلنَّجَوٰةِ وَتَدْعُونَنِىٓ إِلَى ٱلنَّارِ ﴿٤١﴾	40: 41	غافر	ٱلنَّجَوٰةِ
وَمَنَوٰةَ ٱلثَّالِثَةَ ٱلْأُخْرَىٰٓ ﴿٢٠﴾	53: 20	النجم	وَمَنَوٰةَ

It is said that this is based on the fact that some Arab tribes used to pronounce such words with a blend of *wāw* and they would write them with a *wāw* instead of *alif*.[103] The scholars of *ḍabṭ* place a mini *alif* on top of the *wāw* to indicate the pronunciation of the *alif*.

4. *Ibdāl* of *alif* to *yā*ʾ: Such *alifs* are also known as *alif maqṣūrah*. This occurs in many words of the Qurʾān including but not restricted to:

[103] Ghānim Qaddūrī al-Ḥamad, *al-Muyassar*, 224.

هَوى أَوحى أتهم مَولَٰهُم ضحىها تلىها سُقْيَٰهَا فَسَوَّىٰهَا أَشْقَىٰهَا

This is based on the habit of the Arabs in earlier times of writing the *alif* on which *imālah* is made in the form of *yā'* to indicate that *imālah* may be made.[104] Scholars of *ḍabṭ* place a mini *alif* on top of such *yā's* to indicate the pronunciation of *alif* instead of *ya'*.

5. *Ibdāl* of *sīn* to *ṣād* in the following words in their respective *āyāt*:

Verse	Number	Sūrah	Word
مَّن ذَا ٱلَّذِى يُقْرِضُ ٱللَّهَ قَرْضًا حَسَنًا فَيُضَٰعِفَهُۥ لَهُۥٓ أَضْعَافًا كَثِيرَةً ۚ وَٱللَّهُ يَقْبِضُ وَيَبْصُۜطُ وَإِلَيْهِ تُرْجَعُونَ ﴿٢٤٥﴾	2: 245	البقرة	وَيَبْصُۜطُ
أَوَعَجِبْتُمْ أَن جَآءَكُمْ ذِكْرٌ مِّن رَّبِّكُمْ عَلَىٰ رَجُلٍ مِّنكُمْ لِيُنذِرَكُمْ ۚ وَٱذْكُرُوٓا۟ إِذْ جَعَلَكُمْ خُلَفَآءَ مِنۢ بَعْدِ قَوْمِ نُوحٍ وَزَادَكُمْ فِى ٱلْخَلْقِ بَصْۜطَةً ۖ فَٱذْكُرُوٓا۟ ءَالَآءَ ٱللَّهِ لَعَلَّكُمْ تُفْلِحُونَ ﴿٦٩﴾	7: 69	الأعراف	بَصْۜطَةً
لَّسْتَ عَلَيْهِم بِمُصَيْطِرٍ ﴿٢٢﴾	88: 22	الغاشية	بِمُصَيْطِرٍ
أَمْ عِندَهُمْ خَزَآئِنُ رَبِّكَ أَمْ هُمُ ٱلْمُصَۣيْطِرُونَ ﴿٣٧﴾	52: 37	الطور	ٱلْمُصَۣيْطِرُونَ

Though the above words are originally spelled with *sīn*, they are written with *ṣād* because of a practice prevalent among some Arab tribes of reading the *sīn* with a full-mouth (*tafkhīm*) when it is in proximity to ط.[105] Thus, the *sīn* becomes *ṣād*, and was written likewise in the *maṣāḥif* to indicate this *ibdāl*. Depending on which *riwāyah* is being recited, the reciter will read it as *sīn* or *ṣād*. In the Madanī print, when *sīn* is preferred, it is written on top of the *ṣād*, and when *ṣād* is preferred, it is written underneath the *ṣād*.

---

[104] Ibid., 227; al-Dānī, *al-Muqniʿ*, 63.

[105] Pānīpatī, *As-hal al-Mawārid*, 43.

Waṣl and Faṣl وصل و فصل

Joining and Separating

Waṣl refers to writing two words together as one word when, according to *rasm imlāʾī*, they would be written as separate words. *Faṣl* refers to writing two words separately when in other places they have been written as one word, or when according to *rasm imlāʾī*, they are normally written as one word. Another synonymous term for *faṣl* is *qaṭʿ*.

Terms

Maqṭūʿ: A word separated from the following word. Its infinitive is *qaṭʿ* (to separate). Another synonymous term is *mafṣūl* (separated). Its infinitive is *faṣl* (to separate).

Mawṣūl: A word adjoined to the following word even though in reality they are separate words. Its infinitive is *waṣl* (to adjoin).

It is imperative for a Qāriʾ to know those words that are written at times adjoined and at times separated from the following word in the *rasm* of the *Maṣāḥif ʿUthmāniyya*. *Waqf* is permissible only at the end of a word whether the *waqf* is *ikhtiyārī* (optional), *iḍṭirārī* (out of compulsion), *ikhtibārī* (with the intent of testing) or *intiẓārī* (with the intent of combining *riwāyāt*). If the word is separated from the following word, *waqf* will be made at the end of that word without joining it in any manner to the following word. And if the word is adjoined, *waqf* can only be made at the end of the adjoined word.

الحروف المقطعات

The Separated Letters

This refers to the beginnings of certain sūrahs that begin with letters, e.g., الم الر المص

Though they are recited as separate letters, they are written together as one word.

The Vocative يَا

In Arabic, يَا is used as a vocative i.e., حرف النداء. In the Qur᾽ān, it is always attached to the following word. Examples are يبنؤم يأيها يموسى.

هاء التنبيه

The ها Used to Raise Awareness

This ها is always written adjoined to the next word, e.g. هأنتم هذا هؤلاء

ال للتعريف

The Definite Article ال

The definite article الْ in Arabic is prefixed and adjoined to nouns only. *Waqf* is to be made at the end of the word to which ال is adjoined. *Waqf* cannot be made on ال.

أن لّا

*Maqṭū*ᶜ (separated): أَن لَّا
Mawṣūl (adjoined): أَلَّا

All the *ʿUthmānī Maṣāḥif* are unanimous that in the following ten places the word أَنْ is written separated from لَا:

Verse	Number	Sūrah
وَعَلَى ٱلثَّلَٰثَةِ ٱلَّذِينَ خُلِّفُواْ حَتَّىٰٓ إِذَا ضَاقَتْ عَلَيْهِمُ ٱلْأَرْضُ بِمَا رَحُبَتْ وَضَاقَتْ عَلَيْهِمْ أَنفُسُهُمْ وَظَنُّوٓاْ أَن لَّا مَلْجَأَ مِنَ ٱللَّهِ إِلَّآ إِلَيْهِ ثُمَّ تَابَ عَلَيْهِمْ لِيَتُوبُوٓاْۚ إِنَّ ٱللَّهَ هُوَ ٱلتَّوَّابُ ٱلرَّحِيمُ ١١٨	9: 118	التوبة
فَإِلَّمْ يَسْتَجِيبُواْ لَكُمْ فَٱعْلَمُوٓاْ أَنَّمَآ أُنزِلَ بِعِلْمِ ٱللَّهِ وَأَن لَّآ إِلَٰهَ إِلَّا هُوَۖ فَهَلْ أَنتُم مُّسْلِمُونَ ١٤	11: 14	هود
أَلَمْ أَعْهَدْ إِلَيْكُمْ يَٰبَنِىٓ ءَادَمَ أَن لَّا تَعْبُدُواْ ٱلشَّيْطَٰنَۖ إِنَّهُۥ لَكُمْ عَدُوٌّ مُّبِينٌ ٦٠	36: 60	يس
أَن لَّا تَعْبُدُوٓاْ إِلَّا ٱللَّهَۖ إِنِّىٓ أَخَافُ عَلَيْكُمْ عَذَابَ يَوْمٍ أَلِيمٍ ٢٦	11: 26	هود
يَٰٓأَيُّهَا ٱلنَّبِىُّ إِذَا جَآءَكَ ٱلْمُؤْمِنَٰتُ يُبَايِعْنَكَ عَلَىٰٓ أَن لَّا يُشْرِكْنَ بِٱللَّهِ شَيْـًٔا وَلَا يَسْرِقْنَ وَلَا يَزْنِينَ وَلَا يَقْتُلْنَ أَوْلَٰدَهُنَّ وَلَا يَأْتِينَ بِبُهْتَٰنٍ يَفْتَرِينَهُۥ بَيْنَ أَيْدِيهِنَّ وَأَرْجُلِهِنَّ وَلَا يَعْصِينَكَ فِى مَعْرُوفٍ فَبَايِعْهُنَّ وَٱسْتَغْفِرْ لَهُنَّ ٱللَّهَۖ إِنَّ ٱللَّهَ غَفُورٌ رَّحِيمٌ ١٢	60: 12	الممتحنة
وَإِذْ بَوَّأْنَا لِإِبْرَٰهِيمَ مَكَانَ ٱلْبَيْتِ أَن لَّا تُشْرِكْ بِى شَيْـًٔا وَطَهِّرْ بَيْتِىَ لِلطَّآئِفِينَ وَٱلْقَآئِمِينَ وَٱلرُّكَّعِ ٱلسُّجُودِ ٢٦	22: 26	الحج
أَن لَّا يَدْخُلَنَّهَا ٱلْيَوْمَ عَلَيْكُم مِّسْكِينٌ ٢٤	68: 24	القلم
وَأَن لَّا تَعْلُواْ عَلَى ٱللَّهِۖ إِنِّىٓ ءَاتِيكُم بِسُلْطَٰنٍ مُّبِينٍ ١٩	44: 19	الدخان
فَخَلَفَ مِنۢ بَعْدِهِمْ خَلْفٌ وَرِثُواْ ٱلْكِتَٰبَ يَأْخُذُونَ عَرَضَ هَٰذَا ٱلْأَدْنَىٰ وَيَقُولُونَ سَيُغْفَرُ لَنَا وَإِن يَأْتِهِمْ عَرَضٌ مِّثْلُهُۥ يَأْخُذُوهُۚ أَلَمْ يُؤْخَذْ عَلَيْهِم مِّيثَٰقُ ٱلْكِتَٰبِ أَن لَّا يَقُولُواْ عَلَى ٱللَّهِ إِلَّا ٱلْحَقَّ وَدَرَسُواْ مَا فِيهِۗ وَٱلدَّارُ ٱلْءَاخِرَةُ خَيْرٌ لِّلَّذِينَ يَتَّقُونَۚ أَفَلَا تَعْقِلُونَ ١٦٩	7: 169	الأعراف
حَقِيقٌ عَلَىٰٓ أَن لَّآ أَقُولَ عَلَى ٱللَّهِ إِلَّا ٱلْحَقَّۚ قَدْ جِئْتُكُم بِبَيِّنَةٍ مِّن رَّبِّكُمْ فَأَرْسِلْ مَعِىَ بَنِىٓ إِسْرَٰٓءِيلَ ١٠٥	7: 105	الأعراف

However, the *Maṣāḥif* differ in regards to the following verse:

Verse	Number	Sūrah
وَذَا ٱلنُّونِ إِذ ذَّهَبَ مُغَٰضِبًا فَظَنَّ أَن لَّن نَّقۡدِرَ عَلَيۡهِ فَنَادَىٰ فِي ٱلظُّلُمَٰتِ أَن لَّآ إِلَٰهَ إِلَّآ أَنتَ سُبۡحَٰنَكَ إِنِّي كُنتُ مِنَ ٱلظَّٰلِمِينَ ٨٧	21: 87	الأنبياء

In all other places, these two words are written adjoined (*Mawṣūl*) as أَلَّا.

إِنْ مَّا

Maqṭūʿ (separated): إِنْ مَّا

Mawṣūl (adjoined): إِمَّا

The words إن and ما are written separated in the following verse only.

Verse	Number	Sūrah
وَإِن مَّا نُرِيَنَّكَ بَعۡضَ ٱلَّذِي نَعِدُهُمۡ أَوۡ نَتَوَفَّيَنَّكَ فَإِنَّمَا عَلَيۡكَ ٱلۡبَلَٰغُ وَعَلَيۡنَا ٱلۡحِسَابُ ٤٠	13: 40	الرعد

In all other places, they are written adjoined.

أَمَّا

Maqṭūʿ (separated): أَم مَّا

Mawṣūl (joined): أَمَّا

These two words are written adjoined throughout the entire Qurʾān.

عَنْ مَّا

Maqṭūʿ (separated): عَنْ مَّا

Mawṣūl (adjoined): عَمَّا

These two words are written separated in the following verse only.

Verse	Number	Sūrah
فَلَمَّا عَتَوْاْ عَن مَّا نُهُواْ عَنْهُ قُلْنَا لَهُمْ كُونُواْ قِرَدَةً خَٰسِـِٔينَ ١٦٦	7: 166	الأعراف

In all other places, they are written adjoined.

مِن مَّا

Maqṭūʿ (separated): **مِن مَّا**

Mawṣūl (adjoined): **مِمَّا**

These two words are written separated in the following two verses only.

Verse	Number	Sūrah
ضَرَبَ لَكُم مَّثَلًا مِّنْ أَنفُسِكُمْۖ هَل لَّكُم مِّن مَّا مَلَكَتْ أَيْمَٰنُكُم مِّن شُرَكَآءَ فِي مَا رَزَقْنَٰكُمْ فَأَنتُمْ فِيهِ سَوَآءٌ تَخَافُونَهُمْ كَخِيفَتِكُمْ أَنفُسَكُمْۚ كَذَٰلِكَ نُفَصِّلُ ٱلْأٓيَٰتِ لِقَوْمٍ يَعْقِلُونَ ٢٨	30: 28	الروم
وَمَن لَّمْ يَسْتَطِعْ مِنكُمْ طَوْلًا أَن يَنكِحَ ٱلْمُحْصَنَٰتِ ٱلْمُؤْمِنَٰتِ فَمِن مَّا مَلَكَتْ أَيْمَٰنُكُم مِّن فَتَيَٰتِكُمُ ٱلْمُؤْمِنَٰتِۚ وَٱللَّهُ أَعْلَمُ بِإِيمَٰنِكُمۚ بَعْضُكُم مِّنۢ بَعْضٍۚ فَٱنكِحُوهُنَّ بِإِذْنِ أَهْلِهِنَّ وَءَاتُوهُنَّ أُجُورَهُنَّ بِٱلْمَعْرُوفِ مُحْصَنَٰتٍ غَيْرَ مُسَٰفِحَٰتٍ وَلَا مُتَّخِذَٰتِ أَخْدَانٍۚ فَإِذَآ أُحْصِنَّ فَإِنْ أَتَيْنَ بِفَٰحِشَةٍ فَعَلَيْهِنَّ نِصْفُ مَا عَلَى ٱلْمُحْصَنَٰتِ مِنَ ٱلْعَذَابِۚ ذَٰلِكَ لِمَنْ خَشِيَ ٱلْعَنَتَ مِنكُمْۚ وَأَن تَصْبِرُواْ خَيْرٌ لَّكُمْۗ وَٱللَّهُ غَفُورٌ رَّحِيمٌ ٢٥	4: 25	النساء

However, in the following verse, some [*ʿUthmānī*] *maṣāḥif* have them written separated and some adjoined.

Verse	Number	Sūrah
وَأَنفِقُواْ مِن مَّا رَزَقْنَٰكُم مِّن قَبْلِ أَن يَأْتِيَ أَحَدَكُمُ ٱلْمَوْتُ فَيَقُولَ رَبِّ لَوْلَآ أَخَّرْتَنِيٓ إِلَىٰٓ أَجَلٍ قَرِيبٍ فَأَصَّدَّقَ وَأَكُن مِّنَ ٱلصَّٰلِحِينَ ١٠	63: 10	المنافقون

They are written joined in all other places.

أم من

Maqṭūʿ (separated): **أم من**

Mawṣūl (adjoined): **أمّن**

[These two words are written separated in the following four verses only.]

Verse	Number	Sūrah
أَفَمَنْ أَسَّسَ بُنْيَٰنَهُۥ عَلَىٰ تَقْوَىٰ مِنَ ٱللَّهِ وَرِضْوَٰنٍ خَيْرٌ أَم مَّنْ أَسَّسَ بُنْيَٰنَهُۥ عَلَىٰ شَفَا جُرُفٍ هَارٍ فَٱنْهَارَ بِهِۦ فِى نَارِ جَهَنَّمَ ۗ وَٱللَّهُ لَا يَهْدِى ٱلْقَوْمَ ٱلظَّٰلِمِينَ ﴿١٠٩﴾	9: 109	التوبة
إِنَّ ٱلَّذِينَ يُلْحِدُونَ فِىٓ ءَايَٰتِنَا لَا يَخْفَوْنَ عَلَيْنَآ ۗ أَفَمَن يُلْقَىٰ فِى ٱلنَّارِ خَيْرٌ أَم مَّن يَأْتِىٓ ءَامِنًا يَوْمَ ٱلْقِيَٰمَةِ ۚ ٱعْمَلُوا۟ مَا شِئْتُمْ ۖ إِنَّهُۥ بِمَا تَعْمَلُونَ بَصِيرٌ ﴿٤٠﴾	41:40	فصّلت
هَٰٓأَنتُمْ هَٰٓؤُلَآءِ جَٰدَلْتُمْ عَنْهُمْ فِى ٱلْحَيَوٰةِ ٱلدُّنْيَا فَمَن يُجَٰدِلُ ٱللَّهَ عَنْهُمْ يَوْمَ ٱلْقِيَٰمَةِ أَم مَّن يَكُونُ عَلَيْهِمْ وَكِيلًا ﴿١٠٩﴾	4:109	النساء
فَٱسْتَفْتِهِمْ أَهُمْ أَشَدُّ خَلْقًا أَم مَّنْ خَلَقْنَآ ۚ إِنَّا خَلَقْنَٰهُم مِّن طِينٍ لَّازِبٍۭ ﴿١١﴾	37:11	الصّافّات

[They are written adjoined in all other places.]

أن لم

Maqṭūʿ (separated): **أن لم**

Mawṣūl (adjoined): **ألّم**

[These words will be written separated everywhere they appear in the Qurʾān.]

Verse	Number	Sūrah
ذَٰلِكَ أَن لَّمْ يَكُن رَّبُّكَ مُهْلِكَ ٱلْقُرَىٰ بِظُلْمٍ وَأَهْلُهَا غَٰفِلُونَ ﴿١٣١﴾	6:131	الأنعام
أَيَحْسَبُ أَن لَّمْ يَرَهُۥٓ أَحَدٌ ﴿٧﴾	90:7	البلد

إنّ ما

Maqṭūʿ (separated): إنّ ما

Mawṣūl (adjoined): إنّما

These two words are written separated in the following verse only.

Verse	Number	Sūrah
إِنَّ مَا تُوعَدُونَ لَآتٍ ۖ وَمَآ أَنتُم بِمُعْجِزِينَ ﴿١٣٤﴾	6: 134	الأنعام

They are written adjoined in all other places.

أنّ ما

Maqṭūʿ (separated): أنّ ما

Mawṣūl (adjoined): أنّما

These two words are written separated in the following two places.

Verse	Number	Sūrah
ذَٰلِكَ بِأَنَّ ٱللَّهَ هُوَ ٱلْحَقُّ وَأَنَّ مَا يَدْعُونَ مِن دُونِهِۦ هُوَ ٱلْبَٰطِلُ وَأَنَّ ٱللَّهَ هُوَ ٱلْعَلِيُّ ٱلْكَبِيرُ ﴿٦٢﴾	22: 62	الحج
ذَٰلِكَ بِأَنَّ ٱللَّهَ هُوَ ٱلْحَقُّ وَأَنَّ مَا يَدْعُونَ مِن دُونِهِ ٱلْبَٰطِلُ وَأَنَّ ٱللَّهَ هُوَ ٱلْعَلِيُّ ٱلْكَبِيرُ ﴿٣٠﴾	31: 30	لقمان

However, in the following two places, these two words are written separated in some *ʿUthmānī maṣāḥif* and adjoined in others.

Verse	Number	Sūrah
وَٱعْلَمُوٓا۟ أَنَّمَا غَنِمْتُم مِّن شَىْءٍ فَأَنَّ لِلَّهِ خُمُسَهُۥ وَلِلرَّسُولِ وَلِذِى ٱلْقُرْبَىٰ وَٱلْيَتَـٰمَىٰ وَٱلْمَسَـٰكِينِ وَٱبْنِ ٱلسَّبِيلِ إِن كُنتُمْ ءَامَنتُم بِٱللَّهِ وَمَآ أَنزَلْنَا عَلَىٰ عَبْدِنَا يَوْمَ ٱلْفُرْقَانِ يَوْمَ ٱلْتَقَى ٱلْجَمْعَانِ ۗ وَٱللَّهُ عَلَىٰ كُلِّ شَىْءٍ قَدِيرٌ ﴿٤١﴾	8: 41	الأنفال
وَلَا تَشْتَرُوا۟ بِعَهْدِ ٱللَّهِ ثَمَنًا قَلِيلًا ۚ إِنَّمَا عِندَ ٱللَّهِ هُوَ خَيْرٌ لَّكُمْ إِن كُنتُمْ تَعْلَمُونَ ﴿٩٥﴾	16: 95	النحل

In all other places they are written adjoined.

كُلَّ مَا

*Maqṭū*ʿ (separated): **كُلَّ مَا**

Mawṣūl (adjoined): **كُلَّمَا**

These two words are written separated in the following verse.

Verse	Number	Sūrah
وَءَاتَىٰكُم مِّن كُلِّ مَا سَأَلْتُمُوهُ ۚ وَإِن تَعُدُّوا۟ نِعْمَتَ ٱللَّهِ لَا تُحْصُوهَآ ۗ إِنَّ ٱلْإِنسَـٰنَ لَظَلُومٌ كَفَّارٌ ﴿٣٤﴾	14: 34	إبراهيم

However, in the following verses, these two words are written separated in some ʿ*Uthmānī maṣāḥif* and adjoined in others.

Verse	Number	Sūrah
سَتَجِدُونَ ءَاخَرِينَ يُرِيدُونَ أَن يَأْمَنُوكُمْ وَيَأْمَنُوا۟ قَوْمَهُمْ كُلَّ مَا رُدُّوٓا۟ إِلَى ٱلْفِتْنَةِ أُرْكِسُوا۟ فِيهَا ۚ فَإِن لَّمْ يَعْتَزِلُوكُمْ وَيُلْقُوٓا۟ إِلَيْكُمُ ٱلسَّلَمَ وَيَكُفُّوٓا۟ أَيْدِيَهُمْ فَخُذُوهُمْ وَٱقْتُلُوهُمْ حَيْثُ ثَقِفْتُمُوهُمْ ۚ وَأُو۟لَـٰٓئِكُمْ جَعَلْنَا لَكُمْ عَلَيْهِمْ سُلْطَـٰنًا مُّبِينًا ﴿٩١﴾	4: 91	النساء
قَالَ ٱدْخُلُوا۟ فِىٓ أُمَمٍ قَدْ خَلَتْ مِن قَبْلِكُم مِّنَ ٱلْجِنِّ وَٱلْإِنسِ فِى ٱلنَّارِ ۖ كُلَّمَا دَخَلَتْ أُمَّةٌ لَّعَنَتْ أُخْتَهَا ۖ حَتَّىٰٓ إِذَا ٱدَّارَكُوا۟ فِيهَا جَمِيعًا قَالَتْ أُخْرَىٰهُمْ لِأُولَىٰهُمْ	7: 38	الأعراف

Verse	Number	Sūrah
رَبَّنَا هَٰٓؤُلَآءِ أَضَلُّونَا فَـَٔاتِهِمۡ عَذَابٗا ضِعۡفٗا مِّنَ ٱلنَّارِۖ قَالَ لِكُلّٖ ضِعۡفٞ وَلَٰكِن لَّا تَعۡلَمُونَ ٣٨		
ثُمَّ أَرۡسَلۡنَا رُسُلَنَا تَتۡرَاۖ كُلَّ مَا جَآءَ أُمَّةٗ رَّسُولُهَا كَذَّبُوهُۖ فَأَتۡبَعۡنَا بَعۡضَهُم بَعۡضٗا وَجَعَلۡنَٰهُمۡ أَحَادِيثَۚ فَبُعۡدٗا لِّقَوۡمٖ لَّا يُؤۡمِنُونَ ٤٤	23: 44	المؤمنون
تَكَادُ تَمَيَّزُ مِنَ ٱلۡغَيۡظِۖ كُلَّمَآ أُلۡقِيَ فِيهَا فَوۡجٞ سَأَلَهُمۡ خَزَنَتُهَآ أَلَمۡ يَأۡتِكُمۡ نَذِيرٞ ٨	67: 8	الملك

In all other places they are written adjoined.

بِئْسَ مَا

*Maqṭu*ʿ (separated): **بِئْسَ مَا**
Mawṣūl (adjoined): **بِئْسَمَا**

These two words are written adjoined in the following two verses.

Verse	Number	Sūrah
وَلَمَّا رَجَعَ مُوسَىٰٓ إِلَىٰ قَوۡمِهِۦ غَضۡبَٰنَ أَسِفٗا قَالَ بِئۡسَمَا خَلَفۡتُمُونِي مِنۢ بَعۡدِيٓۖ أَعَجِلۡتُمۡ أَمۡرَ رَبِّكُمۡۖ وَأَلۡقَى ٱلۡأَلۡوَاحَ وَأَخَذَ بِرَأۡسِ أَخِيهِ يَجُرُّهُۥٓ إِلَيۡهِۚ قَالَ ٱبۡنَ أُمَّ إِنَّ ٱلۡقَوۡمَ ٱسۡتَضۡعَفُونِي وَكَادُواْ يَقۡتُلُونَنِي فَلَا تُشۡمِتۡ بِيَ ٱلۡأَعۡدَآءَ وَلَا تَجۡعَلۡنِي مَعَ ٱلۡقَوۡمِ ٱلظَّٰلِمِينَ ١٥٠	7: 150	الأعراف
بِئۡسَمَا ٱشۡتَرَوۡاْ بِهِۦٓ أَنفُسَهُمۡ أَن يَكۡفُرُواْ بِمَآ أَنزَلَ ٱللَّهُ بَغۡيًا أَن يُنَزِّلَ ٱللَّهُ مِن فَضۡلِهِۦ عَلَىٰ مَن يَشَآءُ مِنۡ عِبَادِهِۦۖ فَبَآءُو بِغَضَبٍ عَلَىٰ غَضَبٖۚ وَلِلۡكَٰفِرِينَ عَذَابٞ مُّهِينٞ ٩٠	2: 90	البقرة

However, in the following verse, these two words are written separated in some *ʿUthmānī maṣāhif* and adjoined in others.

Verse	Number	Sūrah
وَإِذۡ أَخَذۡنَا مِيثَٰقَكُمۡ وَرَفَعۡنَا فَوۡقَكُمُ ٱلطُّورَ خُذُواْ مَآ ءَاتَيۡنَٰكُم بِقُوَّةٖ وَٱسۡمَعُواْۖ قَالُواْ سَمِعۡنَا وَعَصَيۡنَا وَأُشۡرِبُواْ فِي قُلُوبِهِمُ ٱلۡعِجۡلَ بِكُفۡرِهِمۡۚ قُلۡ بِئۡسَمَا يَأۡمُرُكُم بِهِۦٓ إِيمَٰنُكُمۡ إِن كُنتُم مُّؤۡمِنِينَ ﴿٩٣﴾	2: 93	البقرة

In all other places they are written separated.

في ما

Maqṭūᶜ (separated): في ما

Mawṣūl (adjoined): فيما

These two words are written separated in the following ten verses:[106]

Verse	Number	Sūrah
قُل لَّآ أَجِدُ فِي مَآ أُوحِيَ إِلَيَّ مُحَرَّمًا عَلَىٰ طَاعِمٖ يَطۡعَمُهُۥٓ إِلَّآ أَن يَكُونَ مَيۡتَةً أَوۡ دَمٗا مَّسۡفُوحًا أَوۡ لَحۡمَ خِنزِيرٖ فَإِنَّهُۥ رِجۡسٌ أَوۡ فِسۡقًا أُهِلَّ لِغَيۡرِ ٱللَّهِ بِهِۦۚ فَمَنِ ٱضۡطُرَّ غَيۡرَ بَاغٖ وَلَا عَادٖ فَإِنَّ رَبَّكَ غَفُورٞ رَّحِيمٞ ﴿١٤٥﴾	6:145	الأنعام
وَلَوۡلَا فَضۡلُ ٱللَّهِ عَلَيۡكُمۡ وَرَحۡمَتُهُۥ فِي ٱلدُّنۡيَا وَٱلۡأٓخِرَةِ لَمَسَّكُمۡ فِي مَآ أَفَضۡتُمۡ فِيهِ عَذَابٌ عَظِيمٌ ﴿١٤﴾	24:14	النور
لَا يَسۡمَعُونَ حَسِيسَهَاۖ وَهُمۡ فِي مَا ٱشۡتَهَتۡ أَنفُسُهُمۡ خَٰلِدُونَ ﴿١٠٢﴾	21:102	الأنبياء

---

[106] These ten places can also be written as *mawṣūl*. However, writing them as *maqṭūᶜ* is preferred. *ᶜAqīlah Atrāb*, l. 247-249; Pānīpatī, *Ashal al-Mawārid*, 142-143.

وَأَنزَلۡنَآ إِلَيۡكَ ٱلۡكِتَٰبَ بِٱلۡحَقِّ مُصَدِّقٗا لِّمَا بَيۡنَ يَدَيۡهِ مِنَ ٱلۡكِتَٰبِ وَمُهَيۡمِنًا عَلَيۡهِۖ فَٱحۡكُم بَيۡنَهُم بِمَآ أَنزَلَ ٱللَّهُۖ وَلَا تَتَّبِعۡ أَهۡوَآءَهُمۡ عَمَّا جَآءَكَ مِنَ ٱلۡحَقِّۚ لِكُلّٖ جَعَلۡنَا مِنكُمۡ شِرۡعَةٗ وَمِنۡهَاجٗاۚ وَلَوۡ شَآءَ ٱللَّهُ لَجَعَلَكُمۡ أُمَّةٗ وَٰحِدَةٗ وَلَٰكِن لِّيَبۡلُوَكُمۡ فِي مَآ ءَاتَىٰكُمۡۖ فَٱسۡتَبِقُواْ ٱلۡخَيۡرَٰتِۚ إِلَى ٱللَّهِ مَرۡجِعُكُمۡ جَمِيعٗا فَيُنَبِّئُكُم بِمَا كُنتُمۡ فِيهِ تَخۡتَلِفُونَ ٤٨	5: 48	المائدة
وَهُوَ ٱلَّذِي جَعَلَكُمۡ خَلَٰٓئِفَ ٱلۡأَرۡضِ وَرَفَعَ بَعۡضَكُمۡ فَوۡقَ بَعۡضٖ دَرَجَٰتٖ لِّيَبۡلُوَكُمۡ فِي مَآ ءَاتَىٰكُمۡۗ إِنَّ رَبَّكَ سَرِيعُ ٱلۡعِقَابِ وَإِنَّهُۥ لَغَفُورٞ رَّحِيمُۢ ١٦٥	6:165	الأنعام
وَٱلَّذِينَ يُتَوَفَّوۡنَ مِنكُمۡ وَيَذَرُونَ أَزۡوَٰجٗا وَصِيَّةٗ لِّأَزۡوَٰجِهِم مَّتَٰعًا إِلَى ٱلۡحَوۡلِ غَيۡرَ إِخۡرَاجٖۚ فَإِنۡ خَرَجۡنَ فَلَا جُنَاحَ عَلَيۡكُمۡ فِي مَا فَعَلۡنَ فِيٓ أَنفُسِهِنَّ مِن مَّعۡرُوفٖۗ وَٱللَّهُ عَزِيزٌ حَكِيمٞ ٢٤٠	2:240	البقرة
عَلَىٰٓ أَن نُّبَدِّلَ أَمۡثَٰلَكُمۡ وَنُنشِئَكُمۡ فِي مَا لَا تَعۡلَمُونَ ٦١	56:61	الواقعة
أَلَا لِلَّهِ ٱلدِّينُ ٱلۡخَالِصُۚ وَٱلَّذِينَ ٱتَّخَذُواْ مِن دُونِهِۦٓ أَوۡلِيَآءَ مَا نَعۡبُدُهُمۡ إِلَّا لِيُقَرِّبُونَآ إِلَى ٱللَّهِ زُلۡفَىٰٓ إِنَّ ٱللَّهَ يَحۡكُمُ بَيۡنَهُمۡ فِي مَا هُمۡ فِيهِ يَخۡتَلِفُونَۗ إِنَّ ٱللَّهَ لَا يَهۡدِي مَنۡ هُوَ كَٰذِبٞ كَفَّارٞ ٣	39:3	الزمر
قُلِ ٱللَّهُمَّ فَاطِرَ ٱلسَّمَٰوَٰتِ وَٱلۡأَرۡضِ عَٰلِمَ ٱلۡغَيۡبِ وَٱلشَّهَٰدَةِ أَنتَ تَحۡكُمُ بَيۡنَ عِبَادِكَ فِي مَا كَانُواْ فِيهِ يَخۡتَلِفُونَ ٤٦	39:46	الزمر
ضَرَبَ لَكُم مَّثَلٗا مِّنۡ أَنفُسِكُمۡۖ هَل لَّكُم مِّن مَّا مَلَكَتۡ أَيۡمَٰنُكُم مِّن شُرَكَآءَ فِي مَا رَزَقۡنَٰكُمۡ فَأَنتُمۡ فِيهِ سَوَآءٞ تَخَافُونَهُمۡ كَخِيفَتِكُمۡ أَنفُسَكُمۡۚ كَذَٰلِكَ نُفَصِّلُ ٱلۡأٓيَٰتِ لِقَوۡمٖ يَعۡقِلُونَ ٢٨	30:28	الروم

However, in the following verse, these two words are written separated in all the Maṣāḥif ʿUthmāniyyah.

Verse	Number	Sūrah
أَتُتۡرَكُونَ فِي مَا هَٰهُنَآ ءَامِنِينَ ١٤٦	26: 146	الشعراء

In all other places they are written adjoined.

أينَ ما

Maqṭūʿ (separated): أينَ ما

Mawṣūl (adjoined): أينَما

These two words are written adjoined in the following two verses.

Verse	Number	Sūrah
وَلِلَّهِ ٱلْمَشْرِقُ وَٱلْمَغْرِبُ ۚ فَأَيْنَمَا تُوَلُّوا۟ فَثَمَّ وَجْهُ ٱللَّهِ ۚ إِنَّ ٱللَّهَ وَٰسِعٌ عَلِيمٌ ﴿١١٥﴾	2: 115	البقرة
وَضَرَبَ ٱللَّهُ مَثَلًا رَّجُلَيْنِ أَحَدُهُمَآ أَبْكَمُ لَا يَقْدِرُ عَلَىٰ شَىْءٍ وَهُوَ كَلٌّ عَلَىٰ مَوْلَىٰهُ أَيْنَمَا يُوَجِّههُّ لَا يَأْتِ بِخَيْرٍ هَلْ يَسْتَوِى هُوَ وَمَن يَأْمُرُ بِٱلْعَدْلِ وَهُوَ عَلَىٰ صِرَٰطٍ مُّسْتَقِيمٍ ﴿٧٦﴾	16: 76	النحل

However, in the following three verses, these two words are written separated in some *maṣāḥif ʿUthmānī* and joined in others.

Verse	Number	Sūrah
وَقِيلَ لَهُمْ أَيْنَ مَا كُنتُمْ تَعْبُدُونَ ﴿٩٢﴾	26: 92	الشعراء
مَّلْعُونِينَ ۖ أَيْنَمَا ثُقِفُوٓا۟ أُخِذُوا۟ وَقُتِّلُوا۟ تَقْتِيلًا ﴿٦١﴾	33: 61	الأحزاب
أَيْنَمَا تَكُونُوا۟ يُدْرِككُّمُ ٱلْمَوْتُ وَلَوْ كُنتُمْ فِى بُرُوجٍ مُّشَيَّدَةٍ ۗ وَإِن تُصِبْهُمْ حَسَنَةٌ يَقُولُوا۟ هَٰذِهِۦ مِنْ عِندِ ٱللَّهِ ۖ وَإِن تُصِبْهُمْ سَيِّئَةٌ يَقُولُوا۟ هَٰذِهِۦ مِنْ عِندِكَ ۚ قُلْ كُلٌّ مِّنْ عِندِ ٱللَّهِ ۖ فَمَالِ هَٰٓؤُلَآءِ ٱلْقَوْمِ لَا يَكَادُونَ يَفْقَهُونَ حَدِيثًا ﴿٧٨﴾	4: 78	النساء

In all other places they are written separated.

إن لَّم

Maqṭūʿ (separated): إن لَّم

Mawṣūl (adjoined): إلَّم

These two words are written adjoined in the following verse only.

Verse	Number	Sūrah
فَإِلَّمْ يَسْتَجِيبُواْ لَكُمْ فَٱعْلَمُوٓاْ أَنَّمَآ أُنزِلَ بِعِلْمِ ٱللَّهِ وَأَن لَّآ إِلَٰهَ إِلَّا هُوَ ۖ فَهَلْ أَنتُم مُّسْلِمُونَ ﴿١٤﴾	11: 14	هود

In all other places both words are written separated.

أن لَّن

*Maqṭū*ʿ (separated): **أن لَّن**

Mawṣūl (adjoined): **أَلَّن**

These two words are written adjoined in the following two verses.

Verse	Number	Sūrah
وَعُرِضُواْ عَلَىٰ رَبِّكَ صَفًّا لَّقَدْ جِئْتُمُونَا كَمَا خَلَقْنَٰكُمْ أَوَّلَ مَرَّةٍۭ ۚ بَلْ زَعَمْتُمْ أَلَّن نَّجْعَلَ لَكُم مَّوْعِدًا ﴿٤٨﴾	18: 48	الكهف
أَيَحْسَبُ ٱلْإِنسَٰنُ أَلَّن نَّجْمَعَ عِظَامَهُۥ ﴿٣﴾	75: 3	القيامة

In all other places both words are written separated.

كَيْ لا

Maqṭūʿ (separated): كَيْ لا

Mawṣūl (adjoined): كَيْلا

These two words are written adjoined in the following four verses.

Verse	Number	Sūrah
إِذْ تُصْعِدُونَ وَلَا تَلْوُۥنَ عَلَىٰٓ أَحَدٍ وَٱلرَّسُولُ يَدْعُوكُمْ فِىٓ أُخْرَىٰكُمْ فَأَثَٰبَكُمْ غَمًّۢا بِغَمٍّ لِّكَيْلَا تَحْزَنُوا۟ عَلَىٰ مَا فَاتَكُمْ وَلَا مَآ أَصَٰبَكُمْ ۗ وَٱللَّهُ خَبِيرٌۢ بِمَا تَعْمَلُونَ ﴿١٥٣﴾	3: 153	آل عمران
لِّكَيْلَا تَأْسَوْا۟ عَلَىٰ مَا فَاتَكُمْ وَلَا تَفْرَحُوا۟ بِمَآ ءَاتَىٰكُمْ ۗ وَٱللَّهُ لَا يُحِبُّ كُلَّ مُخْتَالٍ فَخُورٍ ﴿٢٣﴾	57: 23	الحديد
يَٰٓأَيُّهَا ٱلنَّاسُ إِن كُنتُمْ فِى رَيْبٍ مِّنَ ٱلْبَعْثِ فَإِنَّا خَلَقْنَٰكُم مِّن تُرَابٍ ثُمَّ مِن نُّطْفَةٍ ثُمَّ مِنْ عَلَقَةٍ ثُمَّ مِن مُّضْغَةٍ مُّخَلَّقَةٍ وَغَيْرِ مُخَلَّقَةٍ لِّنُبَيِّنَ لَكُمْ ۚ وَنُقِرُّ فِى ٱلْأَرْحَامِ مَا نَشَآءُ إِلَىٰٓ أَجَلٍ مُّسَمًّى ثُمَّ نُخْرِجُكُمْ طِفْلًا ثُمَّ لِتَبْلُغُوٓا۟ أَشُدَّكُمْ ۖ وَمِنكُم مَّن يُتَوَفَّىٰ وَمِنكُم مَّن يُرَدُّ إِلَىٰٓ أَرْذَلِ ٱلْعُمُرِ لِكَيْلَا يَعْلَمَ مِنۢ بَعْدِ عِلْمٍ شَيْـًٔا ۚ وَتَرَى ٱلْأَرْضَ هَامِدَةً فَإِذَآ أَنزَلْنَا عَلَيْهَا ٱلْمَآءَ ٱهْتَزَّتْ وَرَبَتْ وَأَنۢبَتَتْ مِن كُلِّ زَوْجٍۭ بَهِيجٍ ﴿٥﴾	22: 5	الحج
يَٰٓأَيُّهَا ٱلنَّبِىُّ إِنَّآ أَحْلَلْنَا لَكَ أَزْوَٰجَكَ ٱلَّٰتِىٓ ءَاتَيْتَ أُجُورَهُنَّ وَمَا مَلَكَتْ يَمِينُكَ مِمَّآ أَفَآءَ ٱللَّهُ عَلَيْكَ وَبَنَاتِ عَمِّكَ وَبَنَاتِ عَمَّٰتِكَ وَبَنَاتِ خَالِكَ وَبَنَاتِ خَٰلَٰتِكَ ٱلَّٰتِى هَاجَرْنَ مَعَكَ وَٱمْرَأَةً مُّؤْمِنَةً إِن وَهَبَتْ نَفْسَهَا لِلنَّبِىِّ إِنْ أَرَادَ ٱلنَّبِىُّ أَن يَسْتَنكِحَهَا خَالِصَةً لَّكَ مِن دُونِ ٱلْمُؤْمِنِينَ ۗ قَدْ عَلِمْنَا مَا فَرَضْنَا عَلَيْهِمْ فِىٓ أَزْوَٰجِهِمْ وَمَا مَلَكَتْ أَيْمَٰنُهُمْ لِكَيْلَا يَكُونَ عَلَيْكَ حَرَجٌ ۗ وَكَانَ ٱللَّهُ غَفُورًا رَّحِيمًا ﴿٥٠﴾	33: 50	الأحزاب

In all other places, both words are written separated.

عَن مَّن

Maqṭūʿ (separated): عن مَّن

Mawṣūl (adjoined): عَمَّن

These two words are written separated in the following two verses.

Verse	Number	Sūrah
أَلَمْ تَرَ أَنَّ ٱللَّهَ يُزْجِى سَحَابًا ثُمَّ يُؤَلِّفُ بَيْنَهُۥ ثُمَّ يَجْعَلُهُۥ رُكَامًا فَتَرَى ٱلْوَدْقَ يَخْرُجُ مِنْ خِلَٰلِهِۦ وَيُنَزِّلُ مِنَ ٱلسَّمَآءِ مِن جِبَالٍ فِيهَا مِنۢ بَرَدٍ فَيُصِيبُ بِهِۦ مَن يَشَآءُ وَيَصْرِفُهُۥ عَن مَّن يَشَآءُ يَكَادُ سَنَا بَرْقِهِۦ يَذْهَبُ بِٱلْأَبْصَٰرِ ۝٤٣	24: 43	النور
فَأَعْرِضْ عَن مَّن تَوَلَّىٰ عَن ذِكْرِنَا وَلَمْ يُرِدْ إِلَّا ٱلْحَيَوٰةَ ٱلدُّنْيَا ۝٢٩	53: 29	النجم

In all other places both words are written adjoined.

يومَ هُم

*Maqṭū*ʿ (separated): يومَ هُم

Mawṣūl (adjoined): يَوْمَهُم

These two words are written separated in the following two verses.

Verse	Number	Sūrah
يَوْمَ هُم بَٰرِزُونَ لَا يَخْفَىٰ عَلَى ٱللَّهِ مِنْهُمْ شَىْءٌ لِّمَنِ ٱلْمُلْكُ ٱلْيَوْمَ لِلَّهِ ٱلْوَٰحِدِ ٱلْقَهَّارِ ۝١٦	40: 16	غافر
يَوْمَ هُمْ عَلَى ٱلنَّارِ يُفْتَنُونَ ۝١٣	51: 13	الذاريات

لام الجر

*Maqṭū*ʿ (separated): لِ هؤلاء

Mawṣūl (adjoined): وَمَا لِأَحَدٍ

The preposition لِ is written separated in the following four verses.

Verse	Number	Sūrah
وَوُضِعَ ٱلْكِتَٰبُ فَتَرَى ٱلْمُجْرِمِينَ مُشْفِقِينَ مِمَّا فِيهِ وَيَقُولُونَ يَٰوَيْلَتَنَا مَالِ هَٰذَا ٱلْكِتَٰبِ لَا يُغَادِرُ صَغِيرَةً وَلَا كَبِيرَةً إِلَّآ أَحْصَىٰهَا ۚ وَوَجَدُوا۟ مَا عَمِلُوا۟ حَاضِرًا ۗ وَلَا يَظْلِمُ رَبُّكَ أَحَدًا ﴿٤٩﴾	18: 49	الكهف
وَقَالُوا۟ مَالِ هَٰذَا ٱلرَّسُولِ يَأْكُلُ ٱلطَّعَامَ وَيَمْشِى فِى ٱلْأَسْوَاقِ ۙ لَوْلَآ أُنزِلَ إِلَيْهِ مَلَكٌ فَيَكُونَ مَعَهُۥ نَذِيرًا ﴿٧﴾	25: 7	الفرقان
فَمَالِ ٱلَّذِينَ كَفَرُوا۟ قِبَلَكَ مُهْطِعِينَ ﴿٣٦﴾	70: 36	المعارج
أَيْنَمَا تَكُونُوا۟ يُدْرِككُّمُ ٱلْمَوْتُ وَلَوْ كُنتُمْ فِى بُرُوجٍ مُّشَيَّدَةٍ ۗ وَإِن تُصِبْهُمْ حَسَنَةٌ يَقُولُوا۟ هَٰذِهِۦ مِنْ عِندِ ٱللَّهِ ۖ وَإِن تُصِبْهُمْ سَيِّئَةٌ يَقُولُوا۟ هَٰذِهِۦ مِنْ عِندِكَ ۚ قُلْ كُلٌّ مِّنْ عِندِ ٱللَّهِ ۖ فَمَالِ هَٰٓؤُلَآءِ ٱلْقَوْمِ لَا يَكَادُونَ يَفْقَهُونَ حَدِيثًا ﴿٧٨﴾	4: 78	النساء

In all other places the preposition لِ is written as joined.

لاتَ حِينَ

Maqṭūʿ (separated): **لاتَ حِينَ**

Mawṣūl (adjoined): **لاتَحِينَ**

In the *muṣḥaf al-imām*—the *muṣḥaf* ʿUthmān ﷺ had written[107] and kept for himself—the word **لاتَ** is written joined to the word **حين** in the following verse.[108]

Verse	Number	Sūrah
كَمْ أَهْلَكْنَا مِن قَبْلِهِم مِّن قَرْنٍ فَنَادَوا۟ وَّلَاتَ حِينَ مَنَاصٍ ﴿٣﴾	38: 3	ص

There are certain words that are linguistically separate but in the *ʿUthmānī maṣāḥif*, they are considered adjoined in the sense that during *waqf*, it is

[107] By the scribes

[108] It is written as separated in all the other *ʿUthmānī Maṣāḥif*, and writing it is as separated is what is practiced upon. *ʿAqīlah Atrāb*, l. 260. Nādī al-Qiṭṭ, *Hidāyah Uli al-Albāb*, pg. 197.

impermissible to make *waqf* on the first word. Instead, *waqf* will be made on the word following it. For example:

Verse	Number	Sūrah
وَإِذَا كَالُوهُمْ أَو وَّزَنُوهُمْ يُخْسِرُونَ ۝٣	83: 3	المطففين

There is no *alif al-faṣl* after **وَزَنُو** or **كَالُو** to indicate that *waqf* is to be made at the end of **هُمْ**.

وَيْ كَ أَنَّ

These words appear twice in the following *āyah* and are written joined:

Verse	Number	Sūrah
وَأَصْبَحَ ٱلَّذِينَ تَمَنَّوْا۟ مَكَانَهُۥ بِٱلْأَمْسِ يَقُولُونَ وَيْكَأَنَّ ٱللَّهَ يَبْسُطُ ٱلرِّزْقَ لِمَن يَشَآءُ مِنْ عِبَادِهِۦ وَيَقْدِرُ ۖ لَوْلَآ أَن مَّنَّ ٱللَّهُ عَلَيْنَا لَخَسَفَ بِنَا ۖ وَيْكَأَنَّهُۥ لَا يُفْلِحُ ٱلْكَٰفِرُونَ ۝٨٢	28: 82	القصص

وَيْكَأَنَّ in reality is a combination of three words: **وَيْ** and **كَ** and **أَنَّ**. In the Ḥafṣ *riwāyah*, *waqf* can only be made at the end of the third word. According to Imām Abū ʿAmr *waqf* can be made on the **كَ** and according to Imām al-Kisāʾī, *waqf* can be made on **وَيْ**.[109]

[109] *Ḥirz al-Amāni wa Wajh al-Tahānī*, l. 384.

Rules for Writing Hamza According to Rasm ʿUthmāni

Hamz **الهمز**: *Hamz* literally means to prod, urge on, push, spur, and technically it refers to the letter ء because it creates a glottal sound in a word. There are various forms of *hamza*: أ إ ؤ ئ ء ئـ.

Rasm of the Initial *Hamza*

1. At the beginning of a word, *hamza* will always be written on an *alif* as أ if *maftūḥah* or *maḍmūmah* and إ if *maksūrah*, e.g., أقول إبراهيم أنزل. In the South Asian print, the *hamza* at the beginning of a word is written as an *alif* without the small ء on it or underneath it. This is how it was originally written in the ʿUthmānī *Maṣāḥif* as the shape for *hamza* had not been introduced then.[110]

2. The same will apply when there is a particle prefixed to an initial *hamza* as in سأصرف فبأي لبإمام أفأنت.

3. When two *hamzas* come together at the beginning of a word, then, if both are *maftūḥah*, the first will be written as ء, without the *alif* and the second with *alif*, e.g., ءأنذرتهم ءأنت. If the second is *maḍmūma*, the second will be written as a *wāw*, e.g., أؤنزل. If the second is *maksūrah*, the second will be written as a *yāʾ*, e.g., أئنك.

4. The initial *hamza* will not be written as an *alif* if it is followed by an *alif* in order to refrain from writing two *alifs* together, e.g., ءامن.[111] This is the only exception to the rule of writing the initial *hamza* [as an *alif*]. In the South Asian print, this would be written as اٰمَنَ.

---

[110] As mentioned before, the shape of *hamza* is the top part of the letter *ʿain* and was introduced by Khalīl Aḥmad al-Fārāhidī (d. 170 AH).

[111] Al-Ḍabbāʿ, *Samīr al-Ṭālibīn*, 83-84.

Rasm of the Medial *Hamza*

In order to understand this, it is important to know the order of *ḥarakāt* in terms of their strength when on a *hamzah*. *Kasrah* is the strongest, then *ḍammah*, and then *fatḥah*. Also, the preceding letter and its *ḥarakah* will affect how the medial *hamza* is written.

1. If one of the two letters (the *hamza* and the preceding letter) is *maksūrah*, the *hamza* will be written as a *yāʾ* since *kasrah* is the stronger *ḥarakah*. For example, سُئِل فِئَة.

2. If one of the two letters i.e., the *hamza* and the preceding letter, is *maḍmūma* and the other *maftūḥah*, the *hamza* will be written as a *wāw* since *ḍammah* is the stronger *ḥarakah*. For example, فُؤَاد سُؤَال.

3. If both letters i.e., the *hamza* and the preceding letter, are *maftūḥa*, the *hamza* will be written as an *alif*. For example, سَأَلَ رَأَوْكَ.

4. If after the medial *hamza* is an *alif*, the *hamza* will not be written as an *alif* or on any other letter in order to refrain from writing two consecutive *alif*s. For example, مَآبٍ,رَءَا, شَنَآنُ

Rasm of the Final *Hamza*

The final *hamza* will always be written as the long vowel corresponding to the short vowel preceding it.

1. If a *fatḥa* is preceding it, it will be written as an *alif*, e.g., بَدَأَ سَبَأَ
2. If a *ḍamma* is preceding it, it will be written as a *wāw*, e.g., امرُؤ
3. If a *kasrah* is preceding it, it will be written as a *yāʾ*, e.g., قُرئ شَاطِئ
4. If a *sukūn* is preceding it, it will be written without any letter, e.g., مِلْء دِفْء الخَبْء

The difference between *rasm ʿUthmānī* and *rasm imlāʾi* in regard to the *hamza* is mainly based on the following two points:

1. The Arabs at the time of the revelation of the Qurʾān did not have a separate shape for the *hamza* although it was pronounced.[112] They would normally borrow an *alif, yāʾ* or *wāw* to represent it or would omit it altogether from their writing. They would know where and when to recite the *hamza* due to their mastery of the language.[113]

2. The Qurʾān was revealed according to the dialect and accent of some of the tribes that used to make *takhfīf* (creating ease) in the pronunciation of the *hamza*. Thus, the *hamza* would be written according to the long vowel *alif, wāw* or *yāʾ*, whichever was the one that *takhfīf* was in accordance with.

Takhfīf of the *Hamza*

The default position in the pronunciation of *hamza* is *taḥqīq*, pronouncing it from its exact *makhraj* i.e., the furthest part of the throat and with all its qualities. This was the dialect of Hudhail and the majority of Tamīm.[114] However, since the letter *hamza* is the most difficult letter to pronounce due to the distance of its *makhraj* i.e., the furthest part of the throat and due to the qualities of *shiddah* and *jahr*, many tribes, like Quraish and other tribes of the *Ḥijaz*, used to adopt ways of creating ease in its pronunciation.[115] This is known as *takhfīf*.

---

[112] Ibn al-Jazarī, *al-Tamhīd,* 115.

[113] Ibn Ḍiyāʾ Muḥib al-Dīn Aḥmad, *Maʿrifah al-Rusūm*, 5-6.

[114] Al-Ḍabbāʿ, *al-Idāʾah*, 23.

[115] Al-Suyūṭī, *al-Itqān*, 1:340.

Bibliography

Aḥmad, Ibn Ḍiyāʾ Muḥib al-Dīn. *Maʿrifah al-Rusūm maʿa Ḍiyāʾ al-Burhān fī Rasm al-Qurʾān.* Lahore: Qirāʾāt Academy, ND.

al-Azami, Muhamad Mustafa. *The History of the Qurʾānic Text: From Revelation to Compilation.* Riyadh: Azami Publishing House, 2011.

al-ʿĀṣim, Muḥammad Idrīs. *Nafāʾis al-Bayān fī Rasm al-Qurʾān.* Lahore: Qirāʾāt Academy, ND.

al-Masʾūl, ʿAbd al-ʿAliyy. *Muʿjam al-Muṣṭalaḥāt ʿIlm al-Qirāʾāt al-Qurʾāniyyah.* Cairo: Dār al-Salām, 2007.

al-Ḍabbāʿ, ʿAlī. *al-Idāʾah fī Bayān Uṣūl al-Qirāʾah.* Egypt: Al-Maktabah al-Azhariyyah li al-Turāth. ND.

al-Ḍabbāʿ, ʿAlī. *Samīr al-Ṭālibīn fī Rasm wa Ḍabṭ al-Kitāb al-Mubīn.* Egypt: ʿAbd al-Ḥamīd Aḥmad Ḥanafī. First Edition.

al-Dānī, Abū ʿAmr. *Al-Muqniʿ fī Rasm Maṣāḥif al-Amṣār.* Cairo: Maktabah Al-Kulliyāt Al-Azhariyyah, ND.

al-Dānī, Abū ʿAmr. *Al-Muqniʿ fī Rasm Maṣāḥif al-Amṣār wa maʿah Kitāb al-Nuṭq.* Cairo: Dār Ibn Kathīr lil-Nashr wa al-Tawzīʿ, 2018.

al-Dānī, Abū ʿAmr. *Al-Muḥkam fī Naqṭ al-Maṣāḥif.* Damascus: Dār al-Fikr, 1986.

al-Ghazālī, Abū Ḥāmid Muḥammad ibn Muḥammad ibn Muḥammad. *Iḥyā ʿUlūm al-Dīn.* Beirūt: Dār al-Minhāj, 2019.

al-Ḥamad, Ghānim Qaddūrī. *al-Muyassar fī ʿIlm Rasm al-Muṣḥaf wa Ḍabṭih.* Jeddah: Maʿhad al-Imām al-Shāṭibī, 2016.

al-Jaʿbarī, Burhān al-Dīn Ibrāhīm ʿUmar. *Jamīlah al-Arbāb al-Marāṣid fī Sharḥ ʿAqīlah Atrāb al-Qaṣāʾid.* Amman: Arwiqah li al-Dirāsāt wa al-Nashr, 2017.

al-Nawawī, Yaḥyā ibn Sharaf. *Al-Tibyān fī Ādāb Ḥamalah al-Qurʾān.* Cairo: Dar al-Ghad al-Ghadeed, 2019.

al-Qāḍī, ʿAbd al-Fattāḥ. *Tārīkh al-Muṣḥaf al-Sharīf.* Egypt: Maktabah al-Jundī, 1952.

al-Qārī, Mullā ʿAlī. Al-*Minaḥ al-Fikriyyah.* Damascus: Dār al-Ghawthānī, 2012.

al-Qārī, Mullā ʿAlī. *Sharḥ al-Shifā lil-Qāḍī ʿIyād.* Beirut: Dār al-Kutub al-ʿIlmiyyah, 2001.

al-Qiṭṭ, Nādī Ḥaddād Muḥammad ʿAlī. *Hidāyah Uli al-Albāb ilā Sharḥ ʿAqīlah al-Atrāb fī ʿIlm al-Rasm.* Madīnah: Maktabah Dār al-Zamān lil-Nashr wa al-Tawzīʿ, 2012.

al-Suyūṭī, Jalāluddīn. *Al-Itqān fī ʿUlūm al-Qurʾān.* Egypt: al-Hayʾah al-Miṣriyyah al-ʿĀmmah li-l-Kitāb wa al-Ṭabʿah, 1974.

al-Thānawī, Iẓhār Aḥmad. *Al-Jawāhir al-Naqiyyah fī Sharḥ al-Muqaddimah al-Jazariyyah.* Lahore: Qirāʾāt Academy.

al-Zarkashī, Badr al-Dīn. *Al-Burhān fī Ulūm al-Qurʾān*, edited by Maḥmūd Abū al-Faḍl Ibrāhīm. Beirut: Dār al-Maʿrifah, 1957.

Al-Fatāwā al-Hindiyyah. Beirut: Dār al-Kutub al-ʿIlmiyyah, 2000.

Ibn al-Jazarī, Muḥammad ibn Muḥammad. *Al-Tamhīd.* Beirut: Resalah Publishers, 2001.

Ibn al-Jazarī, Muḥammad ibn Muḥammad. *Al-Nashr fī al-Qirā'āt al-ʿAshr.* Beirut: Dār al-Kutub al-ʿIlmiyyah, ND.

Ismaʿīl, Shaʿbān Muḥammad. *Rasm al-Muṣḥaf wa Ḍabṭuhu.* Dār Al-Salām, 2001.

Muḥammad, Nadhar. *Tashīl al-Bayān fī Rasm Khaṭṭ al-Qur'ān* translated by Abū al-Ḥasan Aʿẓamī. Karachi: Maktabah Al-Bushrā, 2013.

Najāḥ, Abū Dāwūd ibn Sulaymān. *Mukhtaṣar al-Tabyīn li-Hijā' al-Tanzīl.* Madinah: The King Fahad Complex for Publishing the Qur'ān, 2002.

Pānīpatī, Fatḥ Muḥammad. *Ashal al-Mawārid fī Sharḥ ʿAqīlah Atrāb al-Qaṣā'id.* Lahore: Qirā'āt Academy, ND.

Pānīpatī, Raḥīm Bakhsh. *Al-Khaṭṭ al-ʿUthmānī fī al-Rasm al-Qur'ānī.* Multan: Idārah Nashr o Ishāʿāt Islāmiyāt, ND.

Sarakhsī, Muḥammad ibn Aḥmad. *Al-Mabsūṭ.* Beirut: Dār al-Maʿrifah, 1993.

Sindī, ʿAbd al-Qayyūm ibn ʿAbd al-Ghafūr. "Muṣṭalaḥ al-Rukūʿ fī al-Maṣāḥif." *Majallah Tibyān lil-Dirāsāt al-Qur'āniyyah.* no. 24 (1437 AH): 19-73.

Qalqashandī, Aḥmad ibn ʿAlī. *Ṣubḥ al-Aʿshā fī Ṣanāʿah al-Inshā'.* Beirut: Dār al-Kutub al-ʿIlmiyyah, ND.

ʿUbaidāt, Maḥmūd Mubarak ʿAbd Allah. "Aṣwāt al-ʿArabiyyah min al-Tartīb al-Abjadī ilā al-Tartīb Al-Ṣawtī." *Majallah Jāmiʿah Dimashq* 29, no. 4+3 (2013): 167-203.

Usmani, Muhammad Taqi. *An Approach to the Qur'ānic Sciences.* Karachi: Darul Ishaat, 2007.

Made in the USA
Columbia, SC
27 May 2024

36225831R00059